Théodore H.

Jicarilla Apaches

Jicarilla Apaches

Gertrude B. Van Roekel

The Naylor Company
Book Publishers of the Southwest
San Antonio, Texas

Copyright ©, 1971 by THE NAYLOR COMPANY

This book or parts thereof may not be reproduced without written permission of the publisher except for customary privileges extended to the press and other reviewing agencies.

Library of Congress Catalog Card No. 73-152304

ALL RIGHTS RESERVED

Printed in the United States of America

ISBN 0-8111-0401-X

Dedicated To
The Jicarilla Apache Tribe
who
in all of life's stages
have taught me
to walk the earth as they walk
to talk to Mother Nature as they talk
and
to be calm and serene in the
climb of life's rocky trail, being
sustained by H O P E

Oh Great Spirit who daily watches us:
As we walk the forest,
We could hear you through the trees;
As we idle near the river,
We hear you talk through rippling —
Oh Great Spirit be with us always;
You are our HOPE that holds us serene.

                        Mrs. Irvin Phone

Preface

The early history of the Jicarilla (pronounced hĭc-ká-rēē-jäa', Spanish for "little baskets" or "little chocolate cup") Apache people are veiled in obscurity, shrouded by pain, sorrow and death; and overshadowed by homeless wandering. This netted a profound loss in lives, homeland and a distinct cultural heritage. However, a binding cohesion maintained a distinct tribe worthy of a "place in the sun" as they were sustained by a dogged determination that averted utter annihilation.

Highlights from the lives of the so-called warring Apaches of Northern New Mexico through the 16th and 17th centuries were woven in this print used as a screen upon which these noble neighbors cast their changing scene. It corrals them from their wanderings on to their homeland. Dulce is the place. Its name "sweet waters" has many more endearing connotations living "at home," "in hope," and toward a bright and promising future.

This pictorial-historical narrative is the answer to the crying need of today's New Indian as he vignettes his past in respect to his adjustment to today's new world with shifting values. It is prepared by request of the Indian people and with their cooperative assistance, spurred on by their keen interest. With thirty years of daily living among the Apaches, observations were first hand, thus the humanitarian aspect has been given due respect.

It was developed, first of all, for the Jicarillas as a fascinating picture album woven into the early events, as well as, chronological history and buildings, many of which have been razed. It also serves as a course for anthropology and sociology classes within the United States and beyond its borders from whence many requests are constantly in demand. It is hoped that today's world sees the Apache as an American citizen with similar strives, ambitions and hopes, thus to be better understood.

Great effort has been exerted to provide scientifically correct data of the years on the reservation along with postdated writings and tales. The historical research, private interviews, and three decades of daily contacts give an insight into the past, the changing aspects of the culture along with a revolutionary adjustment to meet the ways of the late twenties.

Words that were used from the native tongue add color to the Indians' lives. The language is not a written language, so the *Webster's New Collegiate Dictionary*'s pronunciation key was used for the diacritical markings, to give sounds as nearly comparable to the spoken Apache as possible. This was through the able assistance of Cevero Caramillo, Wilma and Irvin Phone, Mary Lou and Melvin Vicenti.

The pictures are collections of former mission employees. Laurels of praise are to Hendrina Hospers (deceased), Marie Van Vuren (deceased), Edna Van De Vrede and Marguerite Rymes. The identification and dates of some would have been impossible were it not for Laell and Emma Vicenti, Buster and Maggie Vicenti, Petklo Garcia, Willie and Avis Julian, Hubert Velarde, and Louise Pesata.

Gratitude to Marina Tiznado on her plant knowledge and use of it, with the able assistance of her daughter Tonita Julian. This was added to bits of sharing from many others through the years. May this manner that they with others share an understand- for tomorrow's life.

Research on chronological data again was a collection over time, but verified and unified with help of Victor and Candanaria Vicenti, Gerald and Winona Vicenti, Charlie, Nossman and Lewis Vigil, Mary Becenti, and Helen Levato.

Gratitude is deeply felt for those who expressed views on the changing culture as they recognize it while living it. This is to Cora Gomez, Martha Jean Naranjo, Sam Elote, Jr., and Raleigh Tafoya. It is in this manner that they with others share an understanding of Apache life. Appreciation for their elders and development of character. In fact, I am indebted to the tribe as a whole in portraying the picture of the Jicarilla Apache.

Technical assistance in statistical information was

gleaned from Branch of Land Operation reports and reproduction of some photos.

Resourceful friends and unprinted monographs have added to the store of knowledge. Eleanor Daggett shared her wealth of writing know-how as well as "Hope" in the success of this production in that there was a message to convey along with a determination to realize the goal.

I am greatly indebted to many threads of life interwoven, even some who have been called "Home" in person but ever with me in spirit.

Gertrude B. Van Roekel
Dulce, New Mexico
August 12, 1970

Contents

List of Illustrations	xiii
Between Two Worlds	xv
Blazing the Trail	1
Apache Homeland — 1887-1912	12
Our Own, Our Land — 1912-1937	28
Acceptance of Western Culture, 1937-62	43
On to a Century Milepost, 1962-1987	61
Footnotes	81
Selected Readings	85

List of Illustrations

Picture section between pages xvi and 1
Page 1 Government-Indian Fair near Dulce, 1915
Display of baskets at Indian Fair
Page 2 Margarita De Dios weaving at the age of 76
Page 3 Goost-cha-du Julian, early basket maker, 1863
Page 4 Dumbbell Classes at boarding school started in 1902-3; school, at right, later, became hospital
Bernice Petago, Rosiland Pesata, Delora and Barbara Vigil learning the new math with manipulations, 1961
Page 5 The Jicarilla Reformed Church and parsonage, 1914, with wild sagebrush in foreground
Dormitory added in 1920; children released from the sanatorium boarded at the mission
Page 6 Rev. and Mrs. J. D. Simms were among first members of the mission staff
Miss Hendrina Hospers, also among first members of the mission staff
Miss Hospers visiting with Mrs. Buckskin Tiznado during home call
Miss Hospers devoted thirty-four years of her life to the Jicarilla Apaches
Page 7 Cevero Camarillo, advisor and attendant at the sanatorium, with his wife, 1920
Tom Thompson's family leaving the new Stover Dormitory

xiii

		Young boys, Irvin Max Phone, Cecil Puerto and Donovan Levato, 1937
		Tim Chino represents all the Jicarilla servicemen of our country
Page	8	Ed Ladd Vicenti in buckskin and feathers, camping at the Government-Indian Fair, 1915
		First Government-Indian Fair exhibit hall; unmarried men stayed here also, 1915
Page	9	School work and Indian products at the Government-Indian Fair, 1915
		Sport in the 1900s; Miss Gunnis, teacher, is on the right
Page	10	Dulce Indian Band, 1913
		Dulce Independent Public School Band, 1970
Page	11	Government School, later closed in 1911
		Present Public School, K-12th grade
Page	12	John Lee Levato, No Tongue Inez, and Sam Elote, police mounties of 1917
		Sam Elote, Jr., of the present day Jicarilla Apache Tribal Police Force
Page	13	First Duly Elected Jicarilla Apache Representative Tribal Council, August 4, 1937
		Present Jicarilla Apache Tribal Council, 1971
Page	14	Ration day: woman with her meat for the month
		Issuance at the slaughter house on ration day
		Laell and Emma Vicenti; agency and hospital workers
		The present public health clinic
Page	15	Perfealio Tafoya, chief and leader to council, 1886
		Howard Vigil, serviceman and family man
		Jonathon Wells served his country, now serves his people
		Troy Vicenti started early; now serving in Vietnam
Page	16	Bow and arrow makers of early 1900s: Zepato Negro and Mason Vicenti
		Mattie Phone Quintana, one of the remaining trainers of good sheep dogs
Page	17	Tourism and big hunts make for a change on the economic horizon
		Stocking the lake with fish — from ranching to tourism, fish and game
Page	18	Ramona Wells, a lovely and delightful Christmas Belle, 1969
		Mahalia Maxine Phone's anticipation is the key for all future leaders, 1964
		What will Owen Phone hear in 1987, the close of the Jicarilla century of Dulce living
		Thomasine Howe is building for the future, as well as for fun
Page	19	Victor M. Vicenti and wife Candanaria Puerto with four of their children, 1942
		Everett Vigil and wife, Nancy Lynch with four of their children, 1966

xiv

Page 20
Roline Vicenti, class of '70, looks to the future and continues with higher education
Lena Chino Vicenti advocated education, but was uneducated herself, 1879
The Past — Dotayo Veneno, 1873
The Future — Gary Vicenti, class of '69

Between Two Worlds

"In truth, our cause is your own. It is the cause of liberty and of justice. . . . It is based upon your own principles, which we have learned from yourselves; for we have gloried to count your Washington and your Jefferson our great teachers. We practiced their precepts with success. And the result is manifest. The Wilderness of forest gave place to comfortable dwellings and cultivated fields. . . . Mental culture, industrial habits, and domestic enjoyments, have succeeded the rudeness of the savage state. We have learned your religion also. We have read your sacred books. Hundreds of our people have embraced their doctrines, . . . practiced the virtues they teach, cherished the hopes they awaken. . . . We speak to the representatives of a Christian country; to the friends of justice; the patrons of the oppressed. And our hopes revive, and our prospects brighten, as we indulge the thought. On your sentence our fate is suspended. On your kindness, on your humanity, on your compassions, on your benevolence, we rest our hopes. . . ."

Cherokee Memorial
to the United States Congress
December 29, 1935

Margarita De Dios weaving at the age of 76

Goost-cha-du Julian, early basket maker, 1863

Dumbbell Classes at boarding school started in 1902-3; school, at right, later became hospital

Bernice Petago, Rosiland Pesata, Delora and Barbara Vigil learning the new math with manipulations, 1961

The Jicarilla Reformed Church and parsonage, 1914, with wild sagebrush in foreground

Dormitory added in 1920; children released from the sanatorium boarded at the mission

Rev. and Mrs. J. D. Simms were among first members of the mission staff

Miss Hendrina Hospers, also among first members of the mission staff

Miss Hospers visiting with Mrs. Buckskin Tiznado during home call

Miss Hospers devoted thirty-four years of her life to the Jicarilla Apaches

Cevero Camarillo, advisor and attendant at the sanatorium, with his wife, 1920

Tom Thompson's family leaving the new Stover Dormitory

Young boys, Irvin Max Phone, Cecil Puerto and Donovan Levato, 1937

Tim Chino represents all the Jicarilla servicemen of our country

Ed Ladd Vicenti in buckskin and feathers, camping at the Government-Indian Fair, 1915

First Government-Indian Fair exhibit hall; unmarried men stayed here also, 1915

School work and Indian products at the
Government-Indian Fair, 1915

Sport in the 1900s; Miss Gunnis, teacher,
is on the right

Dulce Indian Band, 1913

Dulce Independent Public School Band, 1970

Government School, later closed in 1911

Present Public School, K-12th grade

John Lee Levato, No Tongue Inez, and Sam Elote, police mounties of 1917

Sam Elote, Jr., of the present day Jicarilla Apache Tribal Police Force

First Duly Elected Jicarilla Apache Representative
Tribal Council, August 4, 1937

Present Jicarilla Apache Tribal Council, 1971

Ration day: woman with her meat for the month   Issuance at the slaughter house on ration day

Laell and Emma Vicenti; agency and hospital workers   The present public health clinic

Perfealio Tafoya, chief and leader to council, 1886

Howard Vigil, serviceman and family man

Jonathon Wells served his country now serves his people

Troy Vicenti started early; now serving in Vietnam

Bow and arrow makers of early 1900s:
Zepato Negro and Mason Vicenti

Mattie Phone Quintana, one of the remaining trainers of good sheep dogs

Tourism and big hunts make for a change
on the economic horizon

Stocking the lake with fish — from ranching
to tourism, fish and game

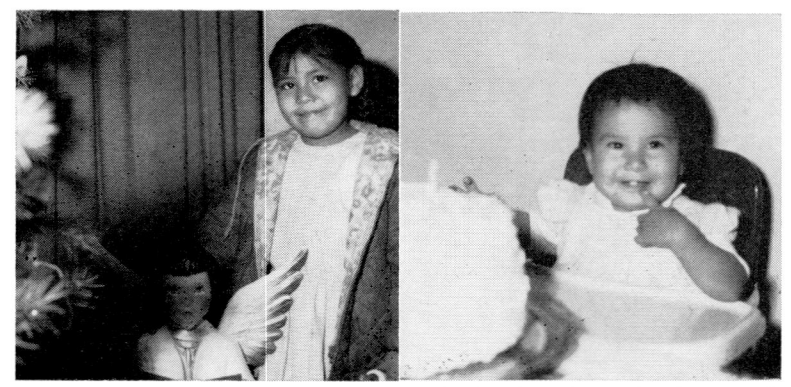

Ramona Wells, a lovely and delightful Christmas Belle, 1969

Mahalia Maxine Phone's anticipation is the key for all future leaders, 1964

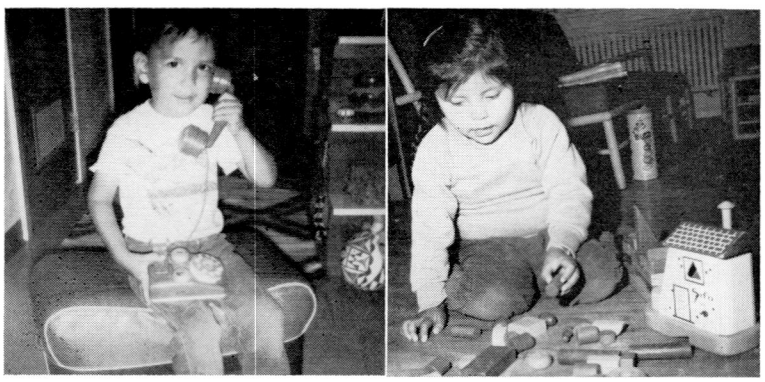

What will Owen Phone hear in 1987, the close of the Jicarilla century of Dulce living

Thomasine Howe is building for the future, as well as for fun

Victor M. Vicenti and wife Candanaria Puerto with four of their children, 1942

Everett Vigil and wife, Nancy Lynch with four of their children, 1966

Roline Vicenti, class of '70 looks to the future and continues with higher education

Lena Chino Vicenti advocated education but was uneducated herself, 1879

The Past
Dotayo Veneno, 1873

The Future
Gary Vicenti, class of '69

Blazing the Trail

"We Rest Our Hopes. . . ."

The little, narrow-gauge D&RG train has blown its whistle. It was approaching Dulce, the home of the Jicarilla Apache. Even as the wheels were screeching to a halt, an Indian sauntered along, en route to the Wirt Trading Post, but was delayed by the train blocking Main Street. One passenger especially noticed this Indian in typical western attire, with an additional adornment of braids dangling from under his broad-rimmed sombrero. Wonder who that was? That thought flickered by as the handful of passengers alighted the wooden platform, greeted by friends or relatives. The train screaked on its way, fading into the canyon ahead, leaving only a trail of black smoke. No, it left this novice of a westerner, who, like the Apaches, was to call Dulce "home." Her desire to run — somewhere — was thwarted by fellow missionaries who were whisking her off to the mission, which also became "home." But, who was this first Apache she saw? Too many thoughts and events flooded her mind now, but, had she gone on to the store, there would have been a score of others resembling him. His only identification now is one of the seven hundred Apaches who resided here three decades ago.

These experiences are written indelibly upon the mind of the author who was introduced to the "Apacheria" at that time (a colloquial expression for their homeland). Since the mind had been colored with historical records, bloody dramas and unruly outbursts, could these gentle, soft-spoken friends be the same? What a paradox until the removal of fear, the feeling of solidarity, and respectful treatment explained the difference. Less than a century ago they were in search of just these elements. They borrowed their names from the neighboring Spanish, they incorporated their dances with the Northern Pueblos, and blended their religion with Catholicism while they were wandering in search of their own. Wandering was not an inherent trait but only a means of sustenance until they had a "home."

The early origin myth rationalized these roamings. The creator, Black Hactcin[a] (hä sh chin') told Ancestral Man (the first man) and Ancestral Woman (the first woman) to stay anywhere they liked as they made their first earthly appearance. "This is your place. Wherever you like to be is your home." This is believed to be the reason for their apparent search. After settling in one choice spot, they would say, "This is pretty; let's stay here," but later would trudge on to another likely spot, at least for a time.

Before they could feast their eyes upon the wooded foothills of the Rockies and grow in the delights of the life-giving Navajo River they were unable to say "This is the place." Less than a century ago they were marauding and pillaging, too busy to record history, so that their early life is veiled in the mist of antiquity. They could only say, "We rest our hope. . . ."[1] A long bitter trail awaited the realization of this hope.

The broken pieces of the Apache history indicate that the last of the tribes to enter the Southwest, the Apaches, were met by Coronado in 1541.[2] Coronado was scouting the area from Mexico in search of the fabled treasures. He reported that they "travel like Arabs with their tents and troops of dogs are loaded with poles and have moorish pack saddles with girths. . . ."[3] Of the travelers the conquistadores wrote, "These people eat raw flesh and drink blood. They do not eat human flesh. They are a kind people and not cruel. They are faithful friends."[4] Contrary to this reputation was Onates' encounter in 1599. Later a friar, Fray Alonso Benavides, who attempted to conquer not only by the sword but by the cross, reported, "It is a people very crafty in war."[5] While the dreaded Apache was seen as a warrior, treacherous and guilty of some of the most heinous tortures, he was misjudged. Even though he gloried in warfare as a vocation, it was not to count a coup or take a scalp. It was their means of livelihood. They wore no war bonnets to record their deeds. These braves fought from behind rocks and were adept at concealing themselves in almost any kind of terrain. Many a soldier fought the Apache all day long and never saw one.[6]

In 1200 A.D. these late arrivals to the Southwest, who were a part of the Athabascans (Athabasca is the name of a midwestern Canadian lake and river) came from the Northwest. They were branded by the singsong Athabascan language, with its three tones which can give different meanings to the same syllable.[7] The derivation of their name *Apache*, from the Tewa (tā'wà) name *Apachu* (ä pâh' chōō), is a matter of controversy. One interpretation of their name is that of "enemy" or "stranger," given by the Zuñi Indians when these Apaches intruded upon their land.[8] Also, from the Jahin (jâh in', a name used for Pueblos) came the term *Apaches de Nabahu,* and this term, "Apaches of the Navajoes," is interpreted as "enemies of the cultivated fields." This term was later carried by the Negthanee (Navajoes).[9] Likewise, Spanish history records the name "Apache" in the closing years of the sixteenth century.[10]

Also, it is presumed that the name "Jicarilla" is derived from the Spanish *jicara,* meaning a chocolate cup used for the measuring of corn or beans for planting, which took on the connotation of a basket where seeds are kept, in the eighteenth century. Jicarilla (pronounced hīc-kȧ-rēē-jäa') is the diminutive term for "little basket," or "little chocolate cup."

This rhythmic sounding word embodies more than romance and the stereotype picture on the screen. The quiet charm that now greets the tourist does not reveal the struggle of the past as the search for food traversed the bison area.[11]

As late as 1931 the Apaches were the least known, ethnologically, of the surviving North American In-

4

dian groups.[12] When they entered the Southwest, and especially in northeastern New Mexico, they brought little more than their sinew-backed bow. The bison fell by the trusty arrow; the meat was for sustenance, the skin for clothing and the tipi (pattern and terminology derived from plainsmen.) Thus the tipi dwellers sought a permanent camping ground to stake their skin tipis (tēpēē) and "be at home."

What a new life dawned when the horse became a part of their life. The mustang was introduced to them by the Spanish, and they became known as the "horse Indians." To them the horse symbolized wealth instead of pesos, so "off to the races" for as many as they could acquire — how? — by trading, stealing or bartering. This also meant they could ride farther into the plains for buffalo.[13] The use of the horse and the *travois* (tipi poles converted into a luggage rack drawn by the horse, formerly by the dog) made them more mobile. These fashionable gigs gave the women and children a seat of honor, since woven baskets were affixed to these poles for the "rumbleseat." While prancing with their steeds the men dashed on for a hunt. By trailing eastward they adopted customs and religious rites from these plainsmen. Along these eastern plains they encountered the Comanches, who became their enemy as they attempted to drive the Apaches back. A similar situation was experienced by the Utahs (Utes) in southern Colorado, but with them the treaty of friendly relations with the Kiowas was severed. The association with the Taos, Picuris and Pecos was their friendship tower as the Apaches settled under it. The hair styling of the Picuris was adopted, their art of weaving was adopted, as well as pottery-making with shiny mica for household use. With these neighbors they conducted annual fairs for trading purposes.[14] The little, woven baskets were produced for an acceptable trade item.

The baskets that were (and are) woven were traditionally deep bowls from ten to thirty inches in diameter and from four to eight inches in depth. Shapes varied for special occasions. Keg-shaped, narrow-necked baskets, lined with piñon pitch, became water jugs and household utensils. The bowl-shaped ones projected importance in ceremonial feasts. The materials used were both sumac *(rhus)* called "ke'n" and willows (*trilobate*) called "k'aī." The sumac is the more popular one, since it has a sheen the willow lacks, and turns into a medium, yellow brown color. The reeds were gathered from low, marshy places; preferably when the twigs were tender. Next came the arduous task of splitting the reed lengthwise into thirds for weaving ribbons. Then the strips were dyed, formerly with native dyes, but later aniline dyes became a convenient substitute. Nature provided the choice: red from the mountain mahogany bark; yellow from the barberry root; and varying shades of brown from numerous sources. The coil stitch was woven around a sturdy, bent framework of willow sticks, shaped as the coiling process continued. A good basket maker was indeed hailed as a craftsman in her own right. The dyed strips were inserted between the natural-colored weaving in geometric design to add beauty and saleableness, as well as vented artistic inclinations of the creator. If the path were continuous, a path of natural-colored reed broke the continuity. This allowed the "cheetin" or evil spirit to leave the basket, and prevented it from casting a spell of ill will upon the household of the artist.

The weaving of the rim into a braided finish held religious significance, which compelled the weaver to complete the edge in one day without the presence of children. The "kä' na stōse" (meaning "basket") thus not only identified this Apache tribe, but featured a way of life.

Although this art continued, the nomadic habits prevailed. The Comanche, because he acquired the horse earlier, with swiftness slashed attacks on the plains to the east. This featured some of the Apache battling from Taos to the Arkansas River. The plainsmen were referred to as the *Llanero* (yä ner yhō', Spanish meaning "plains"). Those who, dogged by hostilities, readily squatted near Abiquiu on the Rio Grande, patterned themselves after the Ollero (ō yer ōō, "mountain people"), who were pottery makers. Some historians combine these two as the Jicarilla tribe. These names followed them through their maneuvers to Dulce. These were only names given them by European associates. By 1846 some of the Jicarillas were reported to be as far east as Pueblo, Colorado, but by 1848 there were no more above the Colorado line. The retreat from the plains dates from 1720 to 1750.[16]

In all these travels the mountains were a refuge, and the canyons the quiet places. While the canyons kept two or more mountains from flowing into one, they also furnished rivers or springs. One in particular gushed forth water — not plain water — but hot water with medicinal qualities. This haven was named "Ojo Caliente" (Spanish for "hot water") and was an easy approach from Abiquiu. It remains a solace to many today who seek physical as well as psychological relief. The older Apaches, likewise, came to boil out after the chill "had left the air." It served as the conference headquarters for leaders and medicine men. Time schedules were not pending, so they would sit for hours, waiting for those thoughts which came best when the sweat was flowing freely. The men were not cognizant of passing hours.[17] They knew no time schedules. They even lacked a word for it in their language, and never needed to create apologies to associates as long as *mañana* was indefinite.

A new day was dawning over the Sangre de Christo Mountains that sheltered these homeless nomads. The government's plan of wardship in 1831 added fear mingled with hope. What did these rumblings in the hills imply? The handwriting on the wall of this new word read, "Indian tribes become domestic dependent nations and their relationship to the United States resembles that of a ward or a guardian." The interpretation of this Great White Father's ruling hand can best be envisioned in the succeeding year.[18] Although some relaxed under the government's protective wing, there were still many restless braves eking out an existence by battling the elements of nature and her inhabitants. The longest war, the war of the Apaches against earlier settlers, began in 1681 and ended two hundred years later. Those labeled as the fiercest of people did not stage massacres until they had been victimized by European settlers. Only when they learned the white man's word could not be trusted, did they begin their long struggle for survival.[19] The Apache story from 1835 to 1886 is one of tragedy and broken faith. As they spread terror through vast areas and endured long chases they fought, with astounding success out of all proportion to their numbers. Not until the final surrender of Geronimo with a few ragged followers near Ojo Caliente to Agent John P. Clum and his forty San Carlos Apache policemen[b] were the wars really ended.[20] The Jicarillas could acclaim no great hero, but Lobo and San Pablo (two chiefs) were given recognition. Mangus Coloradus ("Red Sleeves") played a part in their Mescalero Apache tribe associations to the extent that his name was taken by one who carried it to the Apache reservation in Dulce.[21]

The following events before they found their "home" could be assembled at a glance, were they pictographed on a buffalo hide nailed to a sun-baked adobe wall of the Abiquiu Pueblo. Here is a list:

1846   Territorial days began with Charles Bent appointed as governor and Indian agent, by General Kearny. Jicarillas 100 lodges; 500 souls. Again Jicarillas were squeezed out by hunters and farmers with the result of another one-half century of hard times. Reported as having no permanent home.

1848   Changes came in government control when the Southwest was annexed by the United States.

1851   Fort Union was built for defense against onslaughts of the Apaches. One governor after another led forth soldiers but there was still more trouble. Both Apaches and soldiers were guilty. The basic idea was to move the Indians farther from settlements to reduce the temptation of raids. Apaches rebelled at the reservation idea after roaming freely for a thousand years.

1852   Presents (rations) issued at Abiquiu.

9

1853 Kit Carson, Indian Agent under General Kearny, advocated agricultural schools. Apaches still on the east side of the Rio Grande.

1854 Jicarilla way of life was altered by firewater and the establishment of an agency. They signed a peace treaty in July 1854.

1860 Jicarillas number 950 (including some who earlier roamed under another name).

1861 Agency at Cimarron was on land leased from the Maxwell Grant. Plenty of grain and food; pillaging stopped.

1865 Control of Indians under the military. Attempt to settle the Jicarillas at Fort Sumner a place called Bosque Redondo ("wooded, circular area"), a forty-mile-square tract, failed.

1866 Care of Indians transferred from Department of War to Department of Interior.

1872 Cimarron Agency abolished; most of the Jicarillas sent to Tierra Amarilla ("red earth"), town northwest of Santa Fe.

1873 A council was held at Tierra Amarilla with Chief San Pablo, who said, "I am ready to sign the papers. I hope my grandchildren will have better chances offered them, live like white people and learn to take care of their own affairs." Reservation along the Navajo River to become their assigned reservation.

1875 Continued bloody trail led some to settle at Mescalero.

1881 Last rations[e] issued at Tierra Amarilla, and headquarters moved west to Amargo, abandoned railroad headquarters south of Chama.

1885 There were 721 Jicarillas in Mescalero. Two hundred left Fort Stanton and camped near Santa Fe, as many left the new land.

1887 Returned to the reservation where, meanwhile, other settlers had moved in. "HOME at last. . . . . We rest our hopes."

---

a Hactin (many) are supernatural personifications of the power of objects and natural forces.

b Later an informant included two Jicarilla Apache scouts who volunteered to Agent Clum's troop. The San Carlos Apache is a western tribe of Apaches in eastern Arizona.

c The Apaches pronounced *ration* as "la′ son"; it became a local term for Saturday, the day rations were issued.

Apache Homeland

Reservation Assignment, Adjustment;
1887 — 1912

>As monumental bronze unchanged his look; a soul that pity touched, but never shook; Trained, from his tree-rocked cradle to his feet; The fierce extremes of good and ill to brook Impassive – fearing but the shame of fear – A stoic of the woods – man without a fear. Campbell[1]

This stoic of the woods has now been introduced to his "Apacheria" or "our land." Security under the Great White Father structured an ethnic system cast in the die of tribal bonds. After centuries of nomadism, the reservation bounds ushered in a more peaceful era. The wilderness trails, however, were mirrored in their minds and colored the culture they brought to Dulce. Formerly the Apache young man was taught to rely on himself, casting sideways glances toward the motives of others. The Apaches' survival hinged on their ability to learn from their associates or enemies. For example, Chatto, a famous Apache scout, said that his father gave him this advice:

> My son, you know no one will help you in this world. You must do something. You run to that mountain and come back. That will make you strong. My son, you know no one is your friend, even your sister, father, mother. Your leg is your friend; your brain is your friend; your sight is your friend.[2]

It was under shadow of mistrust that the young man went out to face his world and the fate of his path. Preparedness was his means of survival. His education was in the dexterity of his means of defense, as well as being versed in strategy of the enemy. The Apache would say to his son:

> You must have your arrows and your bow where you can grab them. You must have your knife right beside you. You must have your moccasins right beside you. Be on the alert in peace and war.[3]

The long, weary moons filled with distress were finally setting in the horizon of the past. The last arrow had been shot, and ill treatment had been recorded in blood in the annals of history. To the Apache it was indelibly stamped upon his culture. He had not forgotten that his people were hunted like wild animals and driven into wastelands, with part of their families captured. Through all of this bloody past they became a subdued people, but not without hope.

The new home bordered southern Colorado and was fed by the Navajo River, a tributary of the San Juan River, which rose in the snow-clad Rocky Mountains of Southern Colorado.[4] This nearby seven hundred fifty thousand-acre tract joined their allies, the Utes, to the north, and ran down to their "cousins," the Navajos to the south. They saw this high mountain country tower to nine thousand feet, and lower — in parts — at less than six thousand feet.[5] This afforded a comfortable climate of pleasantly cool summers, offset by cold, rigorous winters. The higher rises were studded with evergreens, which slipped down from the higher, adjoining Carson and Santa Fe forests. These wooded lands added to the beauty and wealth of the land.

From the fertile, green valleys issued streams of pure mountain water. Out of these there flowed some "sweet waters" or *dulce* (Spanish for "sweet"), from which the area received its name. The Indian agency bearing this name was laid under the rimrock of sand hills at the foot of the wooded Rockies.

They entered this future home with a handful of possessions. Those who were fortunate had horses. The elderly and the children of those families took turns riding horseback on the travois. The rest had to walk. Being footsore and weary from rough and rocky trails made an evening campsite welcome. But they could not stay long; the early morning bugle of the military, in command, called for action. No more "Indian time," or move when motivated by inspiration or need. This was "Meh hi känō's" (American) time. What a clamor there must have been in finding reservation settlements. Water was essential to life, so that was always a deciding factor. After the tepees were staked and their horses hobbled they had time to think: What had they brought with them? These strong survivors still had their culture and their religion.

As they scanned the strange countryside with uncertainty, they had supporting background. This was built upon their Creator. The elderly storyteller brought the memory of the Apache origin with him. Thus, seated upon a pelt, leaning upon his bedroll of skins, he repeated the origin myth to any listening ear. It ran through the three-toned, singsong tempo, concerning the world when it was nothing.

In the beginning nothing was here where the world now stands; nothing but Water, Darkness and Cyclone. There were no living people nor creatures except Hactcin. How lonely it was. Oh, yes, the Hactcin were here from the beginning. They had the material out of which everything was created. A living woman was created as Earth and they named her Mother. They made the Sky in the form of a man who was called Father.

In the beginning there were different Hactcins in the underworld from whence they came. The mountains had a Hactcin, the different kinds of fruits each had one. Everything had one. Even though the Jicarilla Apaches were living as in a dream world, they dwelt under the earth; but all was darkness. Everything was perfectly spiritual and holy, just like a Hactcin. In the midst of this darkness Black Hactcin was the leader.

"We lived there for many years. But we do not know how long it was."

Black Hactcin first tried to make an animal. After he made it with four legs he put a tail on it. He looked at it and said, "It looks so strange." Then he spoke to the mud figure, "Let me see you try to use four feet." To his surprise it walked all around. That is why children like to play with clay images.

"I'm very pleased," said Black Hactcin. "I think you can be very helpful to me."

He spoke to the image about the possibility of others coming from his body so he would not be alone.

Black Hactcin had power to do anything so he caused all sorts of animals to come from his newly made creature.

Black Hactcin stood back and laughed at the sight of all these funny looking animals with their different habits. People enjoy the antics of animals today and play with them. They see a hog and laugh at it, saying, "Look at that dirty animal lying in the mud." All the little animals up to the big-horned animals were there. But at that time all the animals could speak. Of course those animals spoke the Jicarilla Apache language.

After the animals brought many questions to Black Hactcin he thought hard, and then decided he must divide them into groups. For food he gave grass to the horse, sheep and cow. "That is what you shall eat," he said. To some he gave brush, to some pine needles, and to others certain kinds of leaves. Because of this they scattered, some to the mountains, some to the desert and others to the plains. After each was in his respective place Hactcin said, "It is well. It looks well to see you in these chosen places."

Then Black Hactcin held out his hand and asked

for water to come. When a drop of rain fell into his palm he mixed it with earth, and it became clay. Then he molded a bird with a head, body, wings and two legs. He spoke to the animal, "Let me see how well you use what I made for you." It looked strange and he didn't know if he would like it, but after it flew back to him Black Hactcin said, "Oh, that is fine!"

"I think you need companions like the animals. That is the only way you will be happy and sing." As the bird flew around and around he grew dizzy. In his daze he saw eagles, hawks and the smaller birds. He circled the air and the images he saw followed him and he knew they were real. Even today birds go in a circle to help them rise into the air.

The birds had the same questions as the animals. Again Black Hactcin made good decisions. As to their places to live, each was allowed to make his own choice. They needed food. Black Hactcin raised his hands to the four winds and Cyclone brought all kinds of seeds into his hands. He liked to tease, so he scattered the seeds and told the birds to eat. When the birds tried to eat the seeds he turned these into worms, flies and grasshoppers. At first the birds couldn't catch them.

Then Black Hactcin challenged them, "It is hard work to get food, but you can do it." Then they all chased the insects and grasshoppers. That is why many birds today use the insects for food and chase the grasshopper around. When this was accomplished he turned to the turkey, "You must be in charge of all these seeds." That is why the turkey has control of the crops now.[a]

That is why the turkey is used for Thanksgiving. It is used for food, but the Indians use the feathers too. Some put a turkey feather in each corner of the field; from the many colors of the turkey came the colored Indian corn.

Birds enjoy water. They flew around and they found a fresh mountain stream from which to drink. While they were drinking he rolled moss into balls that he threw into the stream. This made the birds hop back, because these balls became frogs and fish.

Black Hactcin thought there was room for more birds and animals, but the birds talked him into making a companion for them. They felt Black Hactcin would not always stay with them.

The birds and animals helped. They brought pollen from different plants, and especially from corn. This he mixed with red ochre, white clay, jet, turquoise, and any red they could find.[b] Now when Hactcin thought about what he was going to make, he asked his former images to step back. He did not want them to see this time.

After he turned to the four directions he drew a picture on the ground that looked like his body.[c] He used all of these objects that were brought for various parts of the body. Red ochre for blood, coral for the skin, jet black for the eyes. . . . This was man he was making. To give it life he asked Cyclone to blow into the body, and that gave the image life.

The body first moved, then leaned on one hand, and then stood up. How excited the birds and animals were. Hactcin taught him, and spoke to him four times. First he taught him to speak, then laugh, and next to shout. It was a little harder to teach him to walk, but soon he could do that. Then he even learned to run. There was a loud chorus of rejoicing. Man now knew all about his companions, and understood.

The man was the only human being and he needed a companion. Black Hactcin watched; when the man fell asleep he caused him to dream a pleasant dream. He thought a girl was sitting beside him. When he awoke the dream had come true.

He helped her get up. He taught her like Black Hactcin had taught him. Soon she joined him in walking, talking, running and laughing. Again there was joyful music that filled the air. Their creation seemed complete.[6]

Ancestral Man and Ancestral Woman were their names.

After shifting his position away from the dying embers of the cooling ashes, the old storyteller indicated by motion of his hands (whisking one past the other) the end of his tale; he uttered "dä kōō" ("it is finished"). The little children had long curled into sleeping balls, others nodded their heads after the long endurance test, but there was always one most eager listener. This was one who was destined to step into his grandfather's moccasins some day. He already felt this responsibility was to be his.

Thoughts could not linger long, since daybreak brought many new experiences and tasks. The man still needed to bring home the meat for the family. The bear was left to roam at will, for the Apaches had a special truce with him. As he sat on the hilltop along the trail, awaiting the return of the deer, he could spot other trails. Many wandering "Nä kä' yes" (Mexicans; the word meant "the wanderers") were stalking deer too, but also were seeking ways to obtain more land. They had already staked out the good places on the reservation during the time the Apaches came, left and then were brought back. There never were intimate associations with these earlier peoples, except as good gambling partners.

The men also utilized the wooded areas for homes and fuel. The earlier homes were a miniature form of the A-frame house that later became popular in the camper's world. They dug several feet down into the ground, not for a foundation but for the floor level of the home. This gave protection from chilling winds and battering storms. The little stove was often a converted washtub or metal bucket. Many made little adobe[d] fireplaces, and used the adobe as well to caulk the logs that framed the home. No commercial furniture ever favored these homes. It was made through the ingenuity of the homemakers. They utilized what others discarded; vessels, containers, boards, etc. The root of a tree became a three-legged stool; a box, a cupboard; and a board, a drying rack. These homes were the best they had, but these homes had damp, earthern floors, and no windows, causing poor circulation. These were the hotbeds for disease, especially tuberculosis, which later took its toll.

Spring brought relief, for that meant release from the small, dark dugout to a light, fresh-air tepee. These were the homes built largely by the mother. This conical tent, borrowed from the plainsmen,[e] was made by the craftiness of the women. The travois was now again converted to the framework of the tepee, with a patchwork of skins sewed together for the covering. To begin, three poles were tied together at the top and anchored in an upright position, with the skins forming the top, already in place. The distance the bottoms of the poles were spread apart was determined by the amount of covering available, thus making tepees of various sizes. More poles were added for strength, and two outside poles served as supporting flaps for the doorway, and regulated the draft. Later, when canvas could be obtained, the skins were replaced. Large tepees required fifty to ninety yards of material sewed and stretched over the poles. No "Simplicity" pattern was available, but the little seamstress measured the lengths from the bottom up, going to the top in a conical shape. The bottom was stretched and pegged to the stakes that supported the poles. The new home was built.

What a hodgepodge this early settlement must have been. One certainty prevailed, and that was that they chose their neighbors not for reasons of friendship or status, but on the basis of clanship. There were many subdivisions of the two clans mentioned earlier. These groups huddled in one locality, with the oldest woman the leader of her family. Matriarchal control gave her the whip to crack over her family, and over her in-laws who needed to slip in and be a part of her encampment. The nuclear families each had a home within the extended family group.

All this time the children were having a ball. No school! However, they were in a learning process as the training in the arts of homemaking were instilled. Both boys and girls were instructed in "tracking the deer," in knowing the signs of nature, and were fitted to protect themselves against dangers. Nor was etiquette neglected. If a child misbehaved he was reminded "you must be an orphan, you, you never had a grandfather to tell you how to live." Silence was golden; the faint little voices were seldom heard during an adult conversation. Nothing bypassed the observant eye, but it was under the guise of inattention. They learned how to "look" without attracting attention. To stare was a strong breach of etiquette which demonstrated rudeness.

During these early years some Apaches "were still running." The military in command still had some stragglers to corral. In 1890 there were 721 Apaches. The number was raised to 842 in 1893. More were brought onto the reservation, but the death rate at that time exceeded the birthrate, and there were no health records to keep an accurate total.[7] The turn of the century chalked up 800 on the reservation.

The twentieth century favored these newcomers with some security in view. An agent was their middleman, but he was assigned to the Pueblos as well. His headquarters were not at Dulce so he was not a convenient advisor. In Agent Bullis' report[8] there were nineteen of the approximately two hundred school-age children in the Ft. Lewis industrial school who were doing well. When they returned home they again donned their blankets and moccasins. At that time a boarding school for seventy-five students was recommended. Some families saw education as the answer and could not wait, but attended the boarding school at Santa Fe. John Mills Baltazar related his reaction. "My folks took me to Santa Fe to school [later transferred to Fort Lewis, Colorado]. They had a little clothes tied in a bundle for me. I did not know why I had to go there." His folks returned to their home, and the little boy found solace in his loneliness as he sat beside the irrigation ditch and heard the slight trickling of the water over the rocks. He solved the mystery as he said to himself, "I know now why my folks left me; they thought I was the ugliest one of their children and this was their way of getting rid of me." As he explained later, when his life was far spent, "I know now why they sent me. It was not that I was the ugliest; I had to get ready to become a leader for the tribe. It's a good thing I stayed."

In 1901 a little Methodist mission and day school sprang up just south of Dulce, across the Amargo Arroyo. It served well, but not for long; in ten years it was destroyed by fire and was not rebuilt.[f]

The crying need for medical assistance was answered the next year (1902) when Dr. H. M. Cornell, a sawmill doctor at Edith, Colorado, adjacent to the reservation, came twice a week to relieve the destitute, the downhearted and the dying. The latter, death, the Apaches attributed to witchcraft, and thus beyond human aid. He later became the resident doctor in charge of the sanatorium and hospital. To him the Apaches are greatly indebted, for, through his rigorous health program, the dread tuberculosis was conquered.

In the twentieth century, deep tracks of civilization were firmly planted. The years 1902-1903 must have filled all with curiosity, when the first government school and the little hospital west of it were built.

Strange sights colored the scene as girls in military-type uniforms mingled with the boys in army-style suits, hard, heavy shoes, and flattopped, billed caps which almost drew a salute from those they met. All the children were not in school, since some were physically unable and others were tending sheep in the hills. This apparent absence from the home baffled any legal authority in the form of a truant officer, who scratched off a name that had probably been incorrectly enrolled, and the child remained outside the walls of formal learning.

Some of the agency buildings were being built. Rations continued to sustain the Indians; their land of watered canyons and wooded hills overlooking green, irrigated meadows was becoming "home." Their confidence was soon established with one who was in the area when they arrived. This colorful character had a store in Lumberton and in 1906 began the Dulce "Wirt Trading Post," which offered curios to specialties with the regular open-barreled merchandise of that day. When the Apaches were starving to death, and dying at a tragic rate from tuberculosis, Mr. Emmet Wirt extended them unlimited credit at his trading post, and was thus referred to as the "guardian angel."

The commissary was an important building, just east from the trading post. That building bears evidence of the past as it leans on the bank of the arroyo. Later it was converted into a partial warehouse and tourist information center. Here took place a mad scramble for allotted amounts of food for each family, distributed while local tribal police maintained a semblance of order. Food was first consideration. Beef was slaughtered and issued fresh at a slaughterhouse a mile west of Dulce. With the little campstoves issued the makeshift stoves could be replaced, or one used in the home and the other one in the chûg ä o͞o (brush arbor), where summer cooking was done. Clothing and shoes supplied warmth and comfort. Comfort? Not those oversized, stiff, heavy shoes. How could they quietly stalk a deer? They were polite enough not to refuse them, for the shoes were good bartering items in Lumberton, the town just off the reservation which offered gambling entertainment and the bootlegger's wiles. In 1906 a special feature was added. All the parts were packaged for individual assembling — the early "do-it-yourself kit." When all the parts were supposedly in place they had a wagon. The helpful assistance of Mr. Bob Ewell, the counterpart of an extension agent, gave them confidence to do that job. That did not instill bravery to ride in the contraption, nor were they certain of means to mobilize it. Laell Vicenti related the spectacle as a great sport for the youngsters but not for the men. He demonstrated in a gleeful monologue, "The only horses they dared to hitch to the wagons were those that had been trained to pull those poles. We always waited for the show when a horse refused to be harnessed and reared up landing on the wrong side of the wagon tongue. When this was all straightened out they had to try to make them pull." In a push-back, pull-forward motion, he again chuckled as he visualized the dismay of the men as they failed to get the two horses to go ahead at the same time. Finally, when the horses were trained, the men feared the consquences. "You should have seen how that looked to see the men draw up the driving lines, start the team; but the men were walking alongside the wagon." He also added, "When he did ride in the seat on the wagon, the driver had to learn to use the brake. I can still see one woman tumble off the seat, over the front into the sagebrush because the brake was put on too hard. Oh, they had lots to learn." His wife Emma added, "Later when we went to Pagosa in the wagons we saw cars seesawing through the deep ruts and trying to go past us. I said, I would never ride in something like that; but, here we are. We have nothing else to use, but the car."

In the late 1890s the word "allotment" was a new word to the Indians, later signifying purposeful planning. Before this could be accomplished each allottee needed a name for the census and a land assignment. The sketchy, early census rolls record only a surname of the head of the family. Acquiring a census name was for some a grueling test. For some only an attempt at spelling an Indian name was recorded. Many took names from their neighboring Spanish associates, a favorite president, or from nature. Determining one's age was a wild estimate. One Indian might be asked, "How high were you when you left Cimarron? Could the little boy walk when he left Mescalero?" One can see that the short fellow, and the child as an early walker, were given incorrect birth years. Many used X for the date and month, as did Sol-de-dah: "F - head - X/X/1876"[g]

To these allottees, then, sections of land called allotments were granted. Some portions of land afforded greater opportunities than others, and some families became more progressive by using their gains. By 1909 irrigation systems were established from Dulce, John Mills, and La Jara lakes. Parts of the reservation accommodated sheep while other parts were favorable for cattle grazing. In three transactions, in the years 1907, 1908 and 1940,[9] the south end was added to the northern section of the reservation. It was characterized by sagebrush, chico flats and broken mesas bordered by rimrock, but was lower in altitude and was a favorable grazing section. Until the Apaches became stockmen it was leased to outside stockmen.

The government agents were now assigned to the Jicarillas alone and could devote more time to their needs. The names of Wadsworth, Johnson and Green are recalled by senior Apaches. With their help a source of income was realized in a sawmill south of Dulce, opening in 1911. Extensive logging was done by lumber companies.[10] Dulce was one of the Denver and Rio Grande railroad centers, and railroad ties were bought from the Indians. The scales were located directly in front of the agency.[h]

These related incidents, accomplishments and adjustments mark the first twenty-five years of the Jicarillas at Dulce, and the initial development of their resources.

---

[a] The origin of the agriculture is credited to the turkey.

[b] The list of articles are the chief substances used in the Jicarilla ceremonies.

[c] There are other origin stories, but this is the one chosen by the author.

[d] A name given to local dark, heavy soil that, when mixed with water and sun-dried, served as cement. Often it was mixed with straw and formed into bricks.

[e] Referred to earlier in the historical account. The word derived from the French, meaning to use to dwell.

[f] Distant long building in picture of Dulce in early 1900s.

[g] Taken from 1900 census of the Jicarillas.

[h] The building in the photo of the early Dulce village with the high and wide opening was the railroad scales.

Our Own, Our Land — 1912-1937

> A little while and the Old Indians will no longer be, and the young will be even as white men.
>
> Chief Hiamovi in "The Indian's Book"[1]

The toilsome and tedious tasks of the day were followed by the evening fireside chats. These attracted the whole family and kept a closely knit unit. The grandfather was esteemed because his hoary head indicated wisdom and knowledge, as he conducted "bookless schools." In the absence of the three Rs there were pictures of the past; symbolic designs with either an historical account or a spiritual reminder in view. Truly in these dark days the "storyteller" could foresee that the old men would be no longer and the young men be as white men. I doubt that he envisioned the T.V. for watching "High Chaparral" instead of fireside chats. He did, however, foresee the weakening culture as he saw his young people leave for boarding schools. These young people would return for the summer, but that was not story-telling time. Two of his young men, Juan Quintana and Ben Lee Levato, answered their country's call and left the family circle. As soldiers of World War I they were the "modern Apache scouts." How could they maintain their cultural identity?

The Apaches were joined with nature. How could they cling to this if it were not instilled while they were young? A union with nature derived from a tale such as this:

One time a girl and some children were playing in the arroyo. They dug a hole into the side of the bank. This gave them the idea to play "bear." They called the bear to come out of the cave they had made. To their surprise it came out as a girl, but then would return to the cave. They screwed up courage to call it again and this time it came with arms and legs of a bear. The third time it looked like a bear with a girl's head. The fourth time it emerged as a female bear with the mind of a girl. The bear chased all the children and killed all except her sister. The frightened sister ran home to tell the parents. This infuriated the bear, who could hear, and she killed the parents also. The little girl took refuge under a basket. The frightened, crying girl could not be quiet and the basket moved slightly. This the bear saw, and started to take her life. She pleaded for life and the bear granted it if she would go with her to be her servant in the den. She was safe there but very unhappy. When the bear was sleeping, she ventured outside. Six hunters happened by and she told them her story. In order to escape the hunters took her on a long journey, so the bear could never get her. The hunters and the girl became Pleiades (Big Dipper) in answer to the prayer to the Sky for help.

As the historical myth could not be set apart from nature, so religion is also woven in. In fact the whole culture is one picture, and here they are being considered as separate elements. This is only for clarification. Even the secular matters are guided by this cohesive structure.

The religious life of the Indian was important. The Apache faith was very meaningful. They resorted to prayer and songfests to obtain health, food and a blessing upon life,[2] as well as social gatherings. It accompanied him in life, war, sickness, as in all complexities of life. What a satisfaction! There was always a ceremony that could be performed by the medicine man if the bartering offer of sheep, blankets, etc., would meet his desires. This person with supernatural powers received it as the mantle of an elder member was placed on his shoulders. The younger, chosen one received this, if he accepted the offer, and separated himself for a time to receive training from the one in whose moccasins he was to tread. It meant a grueling test of memory in learning the prayers and songs; purifying the life to obtain the power and persistence to train himself physically for this position. He also bore the heavy responsibility of using this new power properly. When misused it may cause sickness or misfortune. Power misused was the cause of "witchcraft," and for some could be used at will. Many received lesser degrees of this power. Pollen, herbs and feathers were usually at hand for any occasion: when the seed was to be planted, the baby born, the home blessed, children's long hair to be cut, or the spell of an eclipse broken. To the Apache the whole world seemed animate.[3] The streams had "living" water; all living things had "pollen," for this is what gave life. His prayers to the sun did not make him a sun worshipper; but the sun was the symbol of life. His prayers to the east early each morning pointed to his dependence upon the Creator, who held the reins for the new day. The Apache venerated the sun as a father by saying he is a child of the sun; but he lacked the idea of the sun being a rewarder or punisher. On this account the sun is given no special worship, nor a place of worship. He believed that each is fated to die in due time, but the deeds of the life are not taken into account. This explains why the present was important, the past was easily forgotten, and the future held no uneasiness nor fear for him.[4]

The mystic spiritualism was hard for others to understand, but was vital to him. He had a deep and fundamental communication with his supreme being in his reverence. In this profound simplicity he had a deep understanding of nature.

Of the religious customs the Bear Dance was highly valued. This was for curative purposes. One family who felt the pressing need of this ceremony usually discovered three others in need of a cure. Four was their sacred number, so four people were treated by the medicine man for four nights. This was staged in a secluded spot in the woods. A big corral was made of young evergreen trees, open to the east, with a large tepee behind it where the medicine man, family, patient and singers were gathered. Four fires blazed on one side of the corral. The dancing continued four nights to cure the one who was ill, or if there were four it was for all of them. This ceremony was around an animal sand painting drawn by the medicine man; meanwhile, dancing continued in the corral. Men finally came in dressed to represent the bear, which is able to cure the ills. The corn held a special place in the ceremony, in the ceremonial basket. If it proved to be the strength of any other animal, then the cause was laid at that animal's feet. The large attraction was food served throughout the ceremony. Many attended these ceremonies for the social impact. The degree of success in the cure hinged upon the esteem that was held for the Indian doctor.[a]

The "coming out dance" was the debutante's party. The young maiden wore the traditional ceremonial buckskin dress. This set her in a place of distinction during the four-day dance. There was an escort chosen for the maiden. The ceremony was conducted by the medicine man within a large tepee. Again the basket was the center of attraction, for the pollen distribution, the use of corn, and the medicine man's blessing of life, health, and motherhood. This ceremony began in the first quarter of the night, and progressed until sunrise after the fourth night. The guests enjoyed the bounteous supply of food, fun and fellowship, in a beautiful mountain spot chosen by the family.

The third fiesta of significance was the Gō-ghēē-ä fiesta (the name was taken from a corrupted form of the Spanish *cuchillo,* meaning knife or sharp blade).

The relay race, the main event, was laid in the vicinity of Abiquiu, along the Rio Grande. It was by a sharp rock formation that reminded them of a sharp blade, for which the fiesta was named. This fiesta gave thanks for the harvest. Seeds for fertility were placed under the half-buried stones; one on each corner of the racetrack. The clans divided for the race; the Llaneros against the Olleros. The winners of the race won the leadership for their clan for the following year. This became the San Antonio or Stone Lake fiesta when they moved to the reservation. Religious rites accompanied the moving of the four stones that marked the racetrack.

A child's life was steeped in the religious ceremonies. From the day of its birth the grandmother had the responsibility to direct the life of this child. She supervised a fourth-day baptismal ceremony, bathing the baby in a sacred water,[a] and gave the baby an Indian name derived from some characteristic. A ceremony of blessing followed in which the child was bundled in papoose fashion. He was securely bound by a long buckskin thong, to which a blessed, turquoise nugget had been attached. All of this had to be maneuvered without the grandmother seeing her son-in-law (father of the baby). If this happened it would cause blindness. Great emphasis was placed on the child's ability to talk. After that it was given a name for the census. The hair, which had never been cut, was shorn by a parent or grandparent versed in the ceremony. Many times the little, shorn braids were placed in a tall pine tree, which symbolized the height to which the child's life should rise. Many home cures, native herbs and potions helped the child to reach adolescence.

Too numerous to relate were additional religious burial rites of the Apaches. The approaching death rites, death rites, burial rites, and the cleansing rites that followed were directed by the medicine man. A wedding ceremony, a new home, an eclipse, a new crop, called for other chants as blessings or the evacuation of the evil spirit. There was no facet of life that was not intertwined with some phase of religion.

Whatever their primitive beliefs were, it is certain that the Apache was influenced by Catholicism, though few were converted. They could be seen wearing crosses, or branding their trails with crosses. These again were symbols for protection. Myths, also, centered about religious beliefs. They included myths about nature, animals, and birds; they made mention of encounters with Kiowas or Utes, indicating that these were of more recent origin than early northeastern history contributed. Superstitions cause reactions that are difficult for a non-Indian to understand. These myths are vital to the Indian, who had it instilled as a part of his religious teachings.

Not even social customs escaped taboos and direction. In this manner the culture had a strong hold on the individual. One might want to kick the traces of traditionalism, but fears cast by the storyteller held the young people in line. Strict sexual morals kept the flagrant member from casting mythology to the breeze. He did not want to suffer the consequences, nor bear the disgrace of the tribe. One of the early policemen reported that there was only one who dared to appear as a drunk at the fiesta. He was tied to a tree, not only to sober up, but to face the tribe he had disgraced.

Many a young maiden had cast a lover's spell

over the schoolboy she chose as her suitor. It was the girls who made the aggressive moves. A ray of sunlight was connected with love charms, in Jicarilla theory. One way to gain favor of men or the opposite sex was to cast a beam of light on a person by means of a mirror or a shiny object. All these lover's designs were foiled when the parents announced the mate they had chosen.

The marital agreement involved an older man, who might serve as a good helper to the family, or one who was able to bring gifts for the family. It might be a good wagon and team, blankets, yard goods, or attractive trinkets. A bright, new tent added to the encampment of the extended family marked a marriage. Some marriages included a wedding fiesta made by a chosen, older person; the wedding meal was shared with friends. The disappointed maiden endured the plan, in obedience to her elders. However, later in life her chosen one often became her husband.

The Apaches were very fond of sports. These were events in which boys could prove their speed, strength and endurance, which were highly esteemed by all. In their horse races they had the confidence of winning when their horse had the spirits' charm upon him. If these sports were struck by a whirlwind or lightning they were halted, since the evil spirit appeared in each of these natural elements.

All the while, a new scene emerged over the reservation. A red ring around the 1910 calendar demarcated a year of progress. To the boarding school was added a day school at La Jara. A large number of families were clustered there, where a government farm, a store outlet and extension-type headquarters were located. In 1914 there was a plan for converting income from timber sales into sheep payments; and some sheep were issued to the families. There was a placement of cattle in some areas of the reservation. The superintendent reported that this showed hope for future existence.

Medical advance pinpointed the first health survey. The black cloud of tuberculosis brooded over 90% of the tribe. All of the six-year-olds were affected. Had this rate continued, the tribe would have been extinct by 1932. By many they were relegated to the numbers of vanishing Americans. They were "destined to die." The transition to reservation life, closed, dark homes in this colder country, and months of inactivity and extreme poverty spurred the tuberculosis germ to thriving activity. The creeping deathtrap was unfamiliar to the Apaches, who were unable to cope with the disease. The charms of the medicine man drew a greater following than the medical remedies. There was a superstitious omen over these new medicines, which the parents refused to give to their children.

History now recorded a depot as a station for the Denver and Rio Grande train. Telegraph was added, and some telephone lines. The Indians began assuming governmental authority. Not in an ordinary fashion: leaders of family groups were chosen to represent the people in decisions made with government authorities. Eight men, with the "a hen thēē in" ("leader" or superintendent) proved their wisdom equal to the responsibility.

Additional assistance and moral strength was supplied by the Reformed Church Mission. The arrival in 1914 of Rev. and Mrs. J. Denton Simms and Miss Hendrina Hospers opened the mission enterprise for the Apaches. They were encountered by an attitude of despondency.

When Rev. J. D. Simms called on the home of one man he was faced with this remark, "Don't come to me with any of your promises. I have no hope. Let me die!"[5] Confidence was won through diligence and prayer. Over horseback trails Miss Hospers rode to the homes to carry the message of "love," and to relieve suffering when possible. It appalled these new helpers to learn that a group of Americans could be neglected for so long; they were deeply moved that the Indians accepted ministry at all after such isolation and neglect. The Indians' indifference and doubt was expressed as the god's anger being bestowed upon them. If they could only determine whose witchcraft induced this plight. The Indians' confidence was slow in coming to the general public and agency personnel, but rapid paces led to those who made sacrifices for them. They became cooperative as long as their ceremonial practices were not interfered with.

Another institution of mercy was added the same year, when an adequate hospital and staff were provided. The location was on the highway to Lumberton, and within walking distance from the agency.

The next year featured the first Agricultural Fair, uniting the harvest displays and the schoolwork with a parade through the streets. The "Exhibition Hall" was the fifth home west of the agency building. It then housed single, male employees. Dulce Rock also received due attention, for under it stately tepees, wagons, horses and friends dotted the scene. Any such gathering unveiled fiesta costumes, feathered headdress, drums, food and fellowship. It was another occasion for a social gathering.

By 1920 the attitude of the people was one of despair, dejection and shiftlessness. They were broken, subdued and hopeless. They were even disdainful of assistance when it was offered.[6] This was just prior to the date of universal citizenship. A picture printed by Oowikapun expressed the Apaches: "I am in body like an old wigwam that has been shaken by many a storm. Every additional blast that now assails it only makes the rents and crevices more numerous and larger. But the larger the breaks and the openings the more the sunshine can enter in."[7] So sunshine was entering while the blasts of despair were assailing. Mr. Chester E. Farris became the superintendent, and proved to be their real friend. He saw that a bit of their spirit remained. He continued the timber sales, which totalled a half-million dollars,[8] and thus improved the economic situation. The annual per capita income was twenty dollars, plus ration.[9] This was converted into an intensive program of water development, and each family received fifty-four head of sheep. Those who became good sheepmen were issued more as a reward.[10] Cattle also dotted the wooded hillsides and grassy canyons.

Mr. Farris, Mr. Wirt, the trader, and Rev. J. D. Simms together determined the necessary steps in the health situation. The tribe had now dwindled to 558, many of whom were older people.[11] A vigorous health program converted the boarding school into a sanatorium. The mission opened facilities for the education of healthy children. The inmates of the "San" had classes so that they could continue some education.

In 1926 Dr. Cornell became the resident doctor, with a keen insight into the needs of tubercular patients. Bed rest was foreign to Indian philosophy. No matter how weak, they kept on their feet, for a bed patient meant the deathbed. The older Indians believed the doctor's medicine was "stuff to kill them off." The doctor made a hundred-mile trip, and the patient refused his medicine. A child at the mission school had appendicitis, and the doctor wanted to operate. The grandfather of the child, an important medicine man, refused as he stroked his long side mustaches (unusual for an Indian). He worded his decision thus, "If my boy die I will kill the white people." After much persuasion, and after seeing the reaction when the appendix ruptured, the old man consented. He insisted on watching the operation, and stood by the doctor with a loaded pistol at his side. When the operation was completed he said, "The doctor is the biggest medicine man on the reservation, for he take out *chee-tin*. He kill my boy alright, but he bring him back to life; so that is alright." Everyone relaxed as the old gentleman ceded to the doctor's success and relaxed his hold on his pistol. The doctor gave him the appendix in a little bottle of alcohol. Still, grandfather concluded, "The Bad Spirits had been caused by the pills given under the direction of the doctor." Vaccinations were strongly opposed as this practice conflicted with their native beliefs. The Hactcin ceremony could ward off epidemics, so anyone who was vaccinated could not become a masked dancer.

Now the greatest remaining need was the Apaches' civic responsibility. If they were to become a self-respecting unit of society, assistance must taper off to a measure of self-reliance, self-government, and the handling of their own property and affairs. Fortunately the most humble member had self-reverence, and every character was an individual and unique. Without exception a Jicarilla would choose his own hearthstone, return to his own parents and the same environment, no matter how deplorable. From this observation the superintendent determined that improvement must come from that very foundation. But it was uphill all the way. Nothing ever came easy for the Jicarillas.

Could even the gods of nature be against them? The winter of 1931-32 took its toll. The deep snow which fell rapidly fatally trapped many a sheepfold while they huddled together for protection. Those Indians who had moved to the south range, a lower elevation, were able to save a small percentage. Hope held the reins, as one owner said, "But we still has our good ones." With assistance from the tribal fund more sheep were supplied, and the sheep industry continued. They tried again, after 72 percent of the livestock was lost.

The Jicarillas had found themselves, after trudging a long, weary road. The Dawes Act of 1887 embodied a "citizenship policy" for the American Indian. Following training on allotted land they could become unrestricted citizens of their state and nation. The Burke Act of 1906 changed this policy to allow the decision of citizenship to be determined by the president. Also, this act prohibited the sale of liquor to the Indian. Congress as well as the Indians found this "a hard row to hoe." By virtue of these acts some Indians became citizens. In 1924 Congress passed an act declaring all Indians within the continental limits citizens of the United States. New Mexico and Arizona still interpreted their own laws, and voting privileges were still denied.

The Indian Reorganization Act of 1934 opened the door to Indian self-government. A charter of incorporation was issued on June 18, and a constitution became their directive. This was a call for all the natural resources of the reservation — tribal and allotted — to be developed in a way consistent with the principles of conservation and the general welfare of the whole tribe.[12] This contemplated decreasing control by the federal government, and vastly greater self-government by the Indians themselves. The Jicarilla tribe unanimously adopted this plan on 3 July 1937. Truly the Fourth of July was their Independence Day that year. This tribe, acclaimed extremely backward and hopelessly disorganized, proved to be a cohesive unit. Culturally, it was one of the most completely Indian groups in the United States. In one sweep it moved forward into economic security, and to a place among the progressive, advancing tribes.[13] All of these blended efforts brought about an opening of the western culture to them.

The Jicarilla Tribal Council was formed, headed by a chairman. Common-law marriages gave way to the requirements of the state of New Mexcio; the Wirt Trading Post became The Jicarilla Apache Cooperative Enterprise. Compulsory education became effective. Independent support was encouraged by the superintendent. "Take care of your herds and they will take care of you."

---

[a] A complete account of the dance is given in Opler's book on "Myths and Tales of the Jicarilla Apaches."

LITTLE INDIANS SPEAK

People said, "Indian children are hard to teach.
Don't expect them to talk."
One day stubby little Roy said,
"Last night the moon went all the way with me,
When I went out to walk."

People said, "Indian children are dumb.
They seldom make a reply."
Clearly I hear wee Delores answer,
"Yes, the sunset is so good. I think God is throwing
A bright shawl around the shoulders of the sky."

People said, "Indian children have no affection.
They just don't care for anyone."
Then I feel Ramon's tiny hand and hear him whisper,
"A wild animal races in me since my mother sleeps
 under the ground.
Will it always run and run?"

People said, "Apaches never take you in.
Outside their thoughts you'll always stand."
I have forgotten the idle words that People said,
But treasure the day when iron doors swung wide,
And I slipped into the heart of Apache land.

Juanita Bell[1]

Acceptance of Western Culture, 1937-62

It was during this exciting time that I was introduced to "Apache land." Yes, *tanjo* is the greeting of welcome, and one which opened the doors of the homes. Why shouldn't the Apache be proud to have you call in his home? His economic situation now is demonstrated by the cabin or loghouse with a floor, windows, furniture and comforts of which his ancestors only dreamed. Also he had the security of owning the land upon which it stands. Now the reservation was theirs at last.[2] What a release of tension this freedom brought. Apprehension shrouded some leaders; but it was to their advantage and the nation's blessing.

This constituted a "nation within a nation." To many an Indian there was only one place where he belonged — his homeland; made sacred by the ageless sleep of his ancestors; made fruitful by the spirits of his children yet unborn. Here the life-rhythm of the tribe could beat on in unbroken harmony.[3] The cohesion of the group was retained in their cumulative characteristics. An Apache individual operates largely within the context of the group. They tried to erase the trail of tears as they gained confidence in the government and in themselves. The Apache, beset by fear, will follow strong leaders for confidence, and has no admiration for the weak. He had traveled many moons before he saw himself with a future; that he survived at all is a tribute to both his physical and mental stamina. As in the past, the tribe demanded very much of every member, even in the toughest situations; this demand still pulsed through every nerve. The deep insecurity he knew was not within his own soul, but within the rough places he trod, through drought, storm and testings. He took this external insecurity and developed it into inward security, both as an individual and as a member of a group. They now faced transition, a new challenge, a test to see if the new reservation structure could be maintained in a dominant society built on individual enterprise. The Apache now is the "marginal man," on the waning side of his Indian culture while the dominant culture is approaching. This developed before he was educationally and sociologically prepared.

There were differences in values. The Indian held cooperativeness high above competitiveness. Only few dared to step out as leaders, since there would be a breach of friendship between them and their peers. The political, educational or economic leader even faced threats of bewitchment, spells and harm. This new system of democracy required the adventuresome spirit of youth, while the Indian revered age and experience. In the Indian life-style sharing was emphasized rather than acquiring.[4] In the extended family all shared and shared alike, even if one received a check in payment for labor. The extended family sensed the time the check would be issued and were on hand to, "Charge it to Juan, he's my cousin." Only shreds of the ravel-edged check were left for Juan. Such values caused conflicts and misunderstanding as the Apache vacillated between two cultures.

Now under tribal direction and decision, they can decry government transactions. Their men were to make decisions. Attitudes of individuals do not shift rapidly, but the leaders now sat at the conference table with associates varying in color and creed, perhaps even with an Oklahoma Indian, their grandfather's enemy. The winds of the present swept out the past while together they were confronted with the future.

The street scene was also changing. The breechcloth worn over the overalls had disappeared. The ladies, broad, leather, silver-studded belt, which concealed the purse strings, became an item worn by the older women only. No longer did little poorly-clad children cling to their mother's long skirts. The hungry look was gone, since they no longer ate bark from the trees, and herbs to keep alive. Better home conditions prevailed, and dreaded deaths were decreased. They were "dropping the blanket."

To drop the blanket meant to accept western dress. The blanket was very versatile; a wrap by day, a pad for the evening chats, and a covering for the night. It was harder for the men to banish their braids since they carried too much dignity as well as religious significance. The dropping of the blanket was an outward sign of the inward desire for progress. They were ready, with boldness, to interchange experiences with other nations. These emerging Indian societies were to supplement the ancient social groups with modern, cooperative forms. In so doing, they will not become divorced from the societies which formed them. Their role in the future will play the part of lessons drawn from the past.[5] They will live by the virtue of their ancestors.

Great strides were to grow out of the New Deal.[6] Homelife still found the drudgery of tasks a part of a day. One day, water was hauled in barrels on the wagons, dipped from the spring. The following day became washday, unless a fresh supply of wood needed to be hauled to heat the water. The washtub of hot water, propped on a bench, was the "washing machine." Power was elbow grease furnished on a scrubbing board by the women. Early washing machines, hand powered, replaced this tedious task. Later, electric motors took over, which seemed a luxury. In similar fashion, each duty was primitive.

The men continued to take the sheep on the daily trek to cool waters, grassy plots, and then shady nooks to rest during the heat of the day. When fields were to be planted all the family joined in the effort. Mostly dry farming was relied upon. This took the skill of the farmer to determine the right spot. Holes were dug by one person; by another person a fish, if available — or part of one, was dropped into the hole for fertilization; a third person dropped the seed, followed by one who hoed over the hole. They did not dally over the field, but hoped for a few ears of corn at harvest when they returned.

Corn, as in ancient days, is still a favorite. Maize (Indian corn) antedated the oldest of civilizations. It was the most difficult to grow, yet was basic to life. The Indian had domesticated corn when he introduced it to the white man. It was not hybrid corn as known today, but it took the new neighbor over four hundred years to develop that.

Corn held a sacred meaning, as it was a gift of Mother Nature. The women prepared the corn. When the kernel was tender it gave a nourishing, milky substance. Thus it was referred to as "mother." It also was converted into a ceremonial treat when made into a nonalcoholic drink called "gho gth pi e"*(tiswin)*. Shelled corn was soaked, allowed to sprout when spread in the sun, then ground on a *metate* (grinding stone) with a *mano* (hand stone). It was then boiled, strained, and allowed to bubble, which indicates it is ready to drink. This practice is still retained, but on a smaller scale.

The contributions of the Indians were numerous. The potato, bean, squash and pumpkin, to mention a few, are still favorites among the Apaches. They utilize the herbs and seasonal plants. A few that remain popular are: the western berry *(prumus demissa)*; it was eaten raw or crushed and made into paddies to be sun-dried, or boiled as winter-dried fruit. Others treated as such are in the *prumus* classification— wild plum and Juneberry. Wild onion *(allium unifolium)* was eaten raw or fried like domesticated onion. Spinach *(chenopadium album)* was an early-spring green as well as parsley *(umbelliferae fanuli)*; the latter was dried and used for seasoning Indian tea for refreshment. The pressure of time, the trend toward urban living, and the convenience of the supermarket has left the plants largely untouched and the berries to the bears.

The white man's medicine has superceded the native medicine, derived from local plants such as: wild buckwheat *(eriogonum racemosum)*, the root of which cures digestive ills as well as the leaves of watercress *(rorippa — nasturtium-aquaticum)*, larkspur roots *(delphinium novemexicana)*, and wormwood leaves *(artemisia fregida)*. The inside of the amole *(yucca glanca)* will prevent a child to be born from developing into too large a child. Bear grass *(nolina microcarpa)* with a smudge fire is used to allay fright. There is a continuous list, but few surviving members are able to identify these plants.

The Apache did not adopt farming seriously. With the use of the horse he became a better herdsman. With some remaining nomadic traits he could not be a successful farmer and also answer the "call of the drum." In Paul Revere fashion, the messenger announced a "medicine dance" approaching. They must then head for the trail. Crops, garden or fowl would not interfere with the pleasureable occasion, but often the flock was driven, grazing as they traveled.[7] For the most part, his efforts were directed toward utilizing what nature had to offer, rather than try to increase its bounty. Even with the modern mechanical devices the Apache has not become a self-supporting farmer. Hay and grain became the most economical crops, although even these produced mere superficial benefits.

Wrenched from freedom to roam at will, that

Apache tendency has not made the adjustment to civilized standards. The pleasure and immediate satisfaction outwitted the will to deny oneself an immediate desire. They lived for the present. Who was concerned about the future? No one had ever seen it; one may not live that long.

In like manner their financial sense was stymied into filling barns for tomorrow. If there was a fast-earned money in his pocket it burned until used — which was immediately. Cash payments were yet to be experienced, for the credit system issued them coupons, and "books were kept" for them by the trader. Now that the trading post was a tribal enterprise, they were entering the whirlpool of cash buying, saving, and spending, which seemed the chief reason for existence.

The smoking embers of the ancient fires were indeed burning out. Tradition played a great part in history. So, throughout the creeping in of political turmoil, old "bow and arrow" makers still sat peacefully, overlooking the tranquil scene, designing their crafts. The advantages of these weapons over the gun were that: they were not as merciless to the animal; noiselessly their *whirr* yielded its foe; and many a deer was downed without notice by the remaining herd. Also, it created continuous challenge and sportsmanship. As corn was the "mother," the bow and arrow was "father"; because it was the function of the father to protect. So, the male was the sex to wield the bow and arrow. When this weapon finally gave way to gunpowder, the men continued to make them for novelty and for museum pieces.

The new constitution and councilmen also did not alter the placid atmosphere of pastoral life. When it was my privilege to visit the homes as a liaison between the families and the mission school and agency, it included long, extended trips covering homes on the southern part of the reservation. Herdsmen, stockmen and families moved down in the fall, and returned in the spring. When the sun was dropping behind the mountain it was time to accept one of the many offers to spend the night in the home. What a comfort to take in the bedroll, wash up and share the warm meal of *kahzyith* (käh zy ith, Apache for beef stew), tortillas,[a] coffee and dried fruit. This was served by a most gracious hostess on oilcloth, usually spread on the floor as a small table, since the temporary winter homes had only the bare necessities. Their comforts of the established home could not be moved, since they followed the herd. Tents were the most practical shelters, but cabins were also built.

The calendar became a cherished item, and red-lettered days marked it into a running diary. However, when it was time to return north they needed no calendar. Their daily communion with nature was their guide. As one mother said, "We will return when the sun moves to the north a bit more. When it comes over that point there (at the left end of the ridge) that is the time we will go." "Lason" was the one day of the month that was circled with keen interest. The Apache language did not lend itself to the pronunciation of *r*, and *l* replaced the *r*. Thus "ration day" became "lason." All the same to them, it meant the one day of the month they all went to Dulce, with a herder left at the camp. Great preparation preceded these long, winter trips to the cold and deep snow of the northern part of the reservation. By Thursday night all was in readiness. At three in the morning, which was often determined by the position of the morning star, all was astir. The father, bundled in his layers of jackets, cap, scarf, mittens and padded overshoes, stepped out into the frosty morning. The snow crackled under his step as the horses were fed and harnessed. Bales of hay were loaded in the wagon for additional feed and warmth for those who "sat in the back" of the driver's seat. The dogs barked anxiously, joining in the scurry; for, if the wagon was going somewhere, they were going too. Even a yearling colt often trotted alongside the wagon, since it still maintained a close attachment to its mother. Meanwhile a hurried cup of coffee with a quick meal was being prepared while the bedrolls were bundled into the wagon. Why all of this for a trip to town? It meant a forty to sixty-mile trek which found darkness wrapping itself around them before Dulce appeared in the valley. Some became weekend visitors in the community center at the mission or in the home of a relative living in the Dulce area. All this effort embodied keen interest.

This trip entailed a Friday night show at the government school, followed by a late precouncil meeting. As the men discussed the agenda, had its meaning interpreted by the ones gifted with understanding, the women enjoyed their social fest. The school children were allowed to spend the weekend with their parents, so they had much to add. Saturday morning the council meeting was held, and the store was a place to spend time, whether one bought or not. The loafers' benches were kept filled in rotation by the standing and leaning crowd, whenever anyone seated felt compelled to leave. The groceries were checked out behind them while saddles, blankets, and ten-gallon hats hung above them. This tempted them to buy, and their credit went higher. On Sunday many attended the mission church services, then later took their children to the dormitories and prepared for Monday's departure. Lots of news was taken back to the camp, as well as the joys of recalling "older days."

Many a story was relived in these remote homes undisturbed by modern contrivances. Not even a car could reach Grandpa Garfield's home. My car was parked along the highway, and I was taxied in by wagon as early evening was being hemmed in by lightly falling snow. Again the setting for the storyteller was perfect; the evening chores were completed, wood piled neatly and within reach to keep the little wood stove supplied, and the third- and fourth-generation family members and guests were in attention. Garfield Velarde entered the reservation with the tribe in his thirties, bringing scars and memories with him. This early marauder became a historian and legal advisor. He wore a presidential medal awarded him. It was even from a president that he selected his name.

His stalwart frame, despite his age, stretched to an erect position, and his gaze grew distant as he again visualized his early Cimarron country. After a pensive moment he was able to begin. "When our people lived in the Cimarron country, they did not have horses, but often went to Oklahoma and brought back horses. Warriors were chosen for the party." One frail-looking child living with Grandpa's grandmother insisted on going, though not assigned by the tribal leaders. "You see, he often slept late, and he was accused of being lazy. The people did not know that it was because he had been out most of the night practicing. He was running and preparing for endurance."

As the interpreter retold the story Grandpa continued drawing designs in the ashes with his whittling stick. He visualized again the fellow warriors. "They were not to lie back at any time, nor stretch full length on the ground, but to remain in a cramped position. This uninvited warrior paid no attention to that rule and again placed himself as an outcast. Before the warriors were to start out, there was a ceremony, where they all gathered in a circle; but the unclaimed warrior was not wanted; he still joined the circle. The rest were given the blessing of tribe for the journey, but none for him."

More wood was added to the fire, positions on or against bedrolls were shifted, and the ninety-year-old veteran continued, "With as much food as they could carry they started out in gay spirits, with the exception of the frail-looking follower. He followed several paces behind." They advanced over unmarked trails and hills as they avoided dangers. They adjusted their arrows in their handmade quivers as they cast slight slurs upon the little trailing shadow.

The coffee was heated for the evening snack while the events ran on. "The time came that the food ran out. They knew they were in buffalo country. If they could only think of a way to get buffalo meat, it would carry them on their journey. Now was the time for the persistent warrior, who told them he would go ahead, go around a rock, and stick his head out over a high point. When they saw that, they would know he was there, and they could chase the buffalo his way. He promised he would catch them." The old man[a] shook his hoary head, saying, "They did not think that would work, nor that he was able, but they were growing hungry and told him to try. There were seven buffalo that crossed their path, and they drove them over the ridge. The unwelcomed warrior became the hero, for he killed all seven, not letting one escape. Now he was considered a brave and taken into the circle."

With graphic, dramatic movements the story continued while only the adults were still wide awake. "The next proof of his ability was the fleet-footed test. They camped one night, not knowing how far they were from the enemy camp. The brave suggested that he run over during the night. The idea was doubtful, but he ran to the enemy camp and was back by morning. This was a two-day journey. On their first journey they managed to get some horses. Besides horses, on the second journey he captured Oklahoma women, which made him the most honored brave."

A little coffee added to the cup indicated that the story was not ended. It did continue as he mused, "On the third journey he encircled a tepee in which the warrior chief and his family were smoking the peace pipe. There was a little hole in the flap of the tent. Through this the brave touched the warrior, to make his presence known. He named himself 'Punch the Chief.' He was invited to join the circle and smoke the pipe, but this he refused to do; but proceeded to use his arrow against the life of the chief. He escaped, and returned home with more flying honors."

In saddened tone the finale closed with the ending of his life. "On his last journey his own scalp was taken as a prize among the Oklahomas. His own people went into the country, fought and sought until they found the remains of the head, and took it home to smoke through as an honorary gesture toward 'Punch the Chief'."[7]

This tranquil pastoral scene continued until the early fifties, when a slow trend toward urbanization began. Stockmen began to join the labor force and hire others to tend their stock. A sociological change crept in as individual families replaced and extended family relationships and moved into homes in the village. The children outgrew the close affinity for several mothers, fathers, sisters and brothers. All maternal sisters were mothers; paternal brothers, fathers; and cousins, sisters and brothers. They left no orphan without a home and family. Terminology cleared as this pattern changed. Earlier, a dormitory child was requesting permission to go to the store; "I want to see my fadder."[b] I informed him his father was at the south end in the sheep camp. In disgust he persisted, "I don't mean dat fadder, I mean the udder fadder."

"Oh," I begged his pardon, "you are speaking of your uncle; yes, I saw him at the store this afternoon."

That, too, was before the term *baby-sitter* entered their vocabulary, for there was always a member of the extended family available.

Educationally, there was a brighter picture. A little public school was now available for those prefering this to the government school and who were living in the village at the mission facilities. In 1940 two government dorms were opened, and the mission boarding facilities were no longer needed.

Also, the sanatorium was phasing out, and closed two years later. It had rendered its years of service.

This indicated stronger children; and the strength of the tribe rested in its increasingly greater younger generation. Responsibilities were shifting to their shoulders, so they needed the courage, endurance and patience, and a steadfast, personal dignity taught them from their cradle.[9]

Some of this vital education was lost to other children who attended schools not in Dulce. They returned a "part of two worlds."

The "Indian way" could not be reconciled to the "white man's world," and there he was not fully accepted. When the adjustment failed outside the reservation, the easiest recourse was to "return to the blanket," to dependency with no direction in life. His acquired skills were "shelved" for lack of adjustment. Psychologically, the distance between him and his parents widened, as his own ideas were at variance with Indian beliefs and practices.

Did the returnee have to wait for advanced adulthood to accept responsibility? In the dominant culture he is the promising leader. He realized that the undereducated parent was not considered capable in advancing political and economic circumstances. With his gun thrown over his shoulder, his trusty mongrel trailing his heels, he took for the hills. Thus he searched for the answer. The status of his parents was lowering. His own sense of inadequacy was looming before him. He returned without an answer and not even a rabbit to feed the sheep dogs, who returned by night from their herding duties.

With some of these splendid qualities the Jicarilla found his place in the Christian world. The listless attitude of the dying Indian was gone. He now, with firmly planted footing, replaced the spirit of fear with the spirit of love. The spirit of God pulsated the veins as Indian people embodied the Christian religion. The Bible was no longer the "white man's book," but a spiritual guide. Baptism was readily accepted, but partly as a ceremony interpreted as "protection." Love replaced fear, and gave courage to follow these teachings in daily application. The personality was not re-created, but given a personal comfort. Superstition and fear were still burdens that were not easily shaken. As each generation of Indians completed their earthly pilgrimage a bit of their religion was buried. Speaking of the soldiers answering their country's call, a middle-aged man said, "I pray for them in the Christian way and in the Indian way. I don't know which is right." Since the Indian prayers were not thoroughly trusted, a different way was accepted. This waning stronghold tottered under changes, as the individual saw Christianity applied to every facet of life. It called for a personal direction for his individual life.

Even traditional moves came unexpectedly for the soldiers and their families. The young man, often a father, went "over the mountain" to unknown country and a new life. The excitement of war swept him into a whirlwind of Americanization. He knows he is of the oldest generation, but is also a part of today's world, and is supported by this government. He has always answered the call of his country, and thus had to forego his Indian ceremonial days. On the contrary, the popular image of the Indian is that of one decked in feathers as he sings and dances. The true Indian life style is one of a loyal citizen. He re-creates his Indian way of life in a modernized twentieth century version as he lives in two worlds.

Their response to the clarion call did cause Congress to bend over the desk and peel out advantages to the Indians. Out of this Redevelopment Act grew the K-12 Dulce Independent Public School, aided with state support; and training in the Jicarilla arts and crafts shop. But it took the action of 1948 before the Indians in New Mexico were granted the right to vote.

It took a while to seize the meaning of the Land Claim Act, which proved an opportunity to reclaim land seized illegally, when such statements could be proven. At first it carried the impact of termination, which would withdraw government control and wardship. Withdrawal of control had rumbled over Indian lands before, and would spell disaster if it came quickly without due preparation. Since the early 1900s initial steps had already been taken to gradually allow more liberty and control of management. Now the apprehensive Apache was able to say he was more prepared than the generation that preceded him.[10]

The midcentury mark found 935 Apaches on the road to "smoother traveling." The tribal funds, derived from natural resources, oil and gas leases, along with hunting and fishing permits, were deposited. The disbursement of these funds was for tribal benefits, not individuals, at least, not until 1952. Again the Apaches passed the civic test. "After the most careful deliberation, all the Indians made their mineral rights over to the tribe, that whatever riches might be found should be applied to the good of all people."[11] If properly managed, the black gold would help the northern New Mexico Apache Indians to become financial agents.

As a result the tribe established a scholarship fund which supported and encouraged higher education and training. The federal government in 1951 established a relocation program to help Indians become a part of the national economy and a part of American life. The allotted land could not maintain livelihood for the growing tribe; thus the Eisenhower Administration policy encouraged the Indians to leave their reservation, sell their holdings and "join the mainstream of American life."[13]

Until 1954, the economy was based primarily on agriculture and stock raising. Now the trend toward wage economy, supplemented by annual tribal payments from dividends, opened a new scene. To cope with it, education became a vital necessity. As an outgrowth, an adult education program was provided by the government.

Their first security was their land. Now their financial status was their second means of security. These broadening trails led toward assimilation. May it be said that it was the assumed pattern. Assimilation means growing together, or it may be called, "the Melting Pot." On the contrary, Anglo, Spanish, and Indian each largely maintained his own culture. It was determined that assimilation was not the answer. Two cultures do not react alike, no more than two individuals think the same. The Indian has been cooperative instead of competitive in the dominant world. His attitude toward work was to work for pleasure. A feast meant heaps of preparation, but it was for pleasurable results, and so a pleasure to prepare. He finds the dominant world filled with work schedules to save money for some distant, planned vacation. As a substitute for assimilation, the plan was for integration in which one learns from another while maintaining his own identity.

The advantage the Indian has is his rich cultural background. He can add to these the necessary skills which equip him for the new world of work he is entering. When he succeeds, then the Apache is a really educated person.

---

a Term "old man" among the Apaches showed reverence and respect.
b The *th* sound, foreign to the Apache language, became a *d* sound.

On to a Century Milepost, 1962-1987

> Turned by the wind goes the one I send yonder: Yonder he goes who is whirled by the winds; Goes, where the four hills of life and the four winds are standing; There in the winds; Goes, where the four hills of life the midst of the winds, standing there.
>
> — From the Omaha tribe, which is befitting to all tribes.[1]

The history of mankind has been a story of man making changes. The adjustment in his living has permitted him to survive and go forward, in spite of failures and setbacks. This was even in the face of some of the gravest dangers. He has always conquered by tackling these hurdles.[2]

How well the Apache paints this picture in his "journey down into the West."[a] He wanted to die. He hoped to die. Now he is one who changed, adjusted and lived to go forward "to the four winds of life." The American Indian, including the Apache, without exception believes the key to unlock his "New World" is *education*. Without it he would not advance. If there is to be a continual flow of Apache leaders at work on the Jicarilla plans and programs, the youth must be challenged. He needs to have continued hope and courage.

The Apaches now assume the right to determine for themselves the disposition of matters that affect their lives and that of the Dulce community. This is the rebirth of Indian energy and initiative, which was lost during years of despondency and dependency. It is needed in a more subtle way today. Arrows of rapid changes rain upon them, but when taken with dignity, under the power of the self-rule, they come forth as conquerors. Never again will the Jicarilla see his own problem in its old, narrow framework. His horizons broaden as he seeks education and develops skills.

Turn back the calendar sixty years. How different it was from the attitude of schools and training today. Victor Vicenti, a boy of ten, relives his school days in the La Jara day school. As he sat back comfortably in his cosy, little cabin he pointed to the south of it, indicating the spot of his former school. "There was the farmers' building," pointing to the north. As he put another piece of cedarwood in the potbellied stove he added, "This is the stove that was used in the school and the government discarded it, but I'm still using it alright."

He screened his memory for the date of 1910, when he was in school. Adjusting his colorful scarf, he prepared to enjoy telling and demonstrating past experiences. "In those days we didn't study very much. We went to school in the mornings. Then we ate a little lunch our folks sent with us and then ran to those rimrocks," as he waved a wide arc to the west. This man, slight of stature, determined his age then by scanning the distance from the floor to his hand raised in the air, "In those days, I wasn't very big," and laughingly chimed, "I never did get very big, but I went with those big boys to play, 'chasing wild horses,' all over those rimrocks there. We took some wire for a bit and bridle with string — we had lots in our pockets — for the lines." He pictured that hillside alive again with his fellow wild horses and captives as he mused on, "We heard the teacher's bell, but paid no attention. We played all afternoon and came down from the chase when it was time to go home."

Resetting his felt hat, shaped to his personality, to shade his failing eyesight, he went on, "You see the farmer[b] had eight bulls, and we drove those bulls way back into that other canyon and hobbled them. They stayed there for a long time until an old man told the farmer where they were and who did it. He was so mad, but we just were punished one day.

"You see the next year the school closed and we went to the Dulce Boarding School. This was because the teachers quit and they couldn't find others to come out here. Those teachers bought a team of horses and a wagon. They put everything on there, even their dogs, and started down the road looking just like an Indian." Again with a waving gesture he sent them down the trail. "They wanted to go to Oklahoma; I wonder how long it took them."

As his grandson enters school in the late twentieth century he continues to bring his self-image as well. Grandmother does not keep his culture wrapped in a towel until he returns. He brings it with him, and it is woven into the core of his life. His culture, language and dress are recognized.

The instructors realize some students live in one world at home and another world while in school. Under the name of *cultural pluralism* these two worlds are fused into one person. The school staff has come to recognize the differences and resolve them for a student who is preparing himself for the new world. This philosophy of education ceases to force white, middle-class values on all people. The school takes into consideration that some of these children are from the parents who were first-generation students. Thus parents are urged to participate in the activities and learn with the children. Changing her attitude, *shichoo* (shi chōō', Apache for "grandmother"), said to her daughter, an adult student, "Go ahead and learn more; you need it now today."

The Dulce public school and government dormitory have advanced far from Oliver La Farge's picture in *The Enemy Gods,* in which the emphasis was on forgetting Indian culture and becoming a white man. Parents could see little use for the school that unfitted their children for reservation life. This explained reluctance to cooperate with plans laid for them. These earlier philosophies have been replaced with those that recognize the right of Indians to be Indians; To be as they are, while they are becoming. The change was slow while the "fences were still up," and professional positions were not designed for Indians. There was no vision of the Indian in a job "upstairs." The beginning of the seventies beams its blessings upon an uneducated Apache range conservationist, two teachers, a university art instructor, a Bureau of Indian Affairs personnel director, two employment assistance personnel, and one climbing the ladder of law, aside from vocational trainees and tribal leaders holding responsible positions. These jobs were formerly held by his "white brother." By the close of the centenary anniversary (1987) for the Jicarilla reservation,[c] those who are now preparing themselves will be "in the harness."

The Indian people are becoming younger, more educated, more curious and more eager. They no longer can be the Indians their ancestors were. But they continue to be Indian as they plunge into the current stream of American life. No river returns to its source, yet each one has a beginning. Indian youth, like the stream, grows from the source. The strength gained, wisdom acquired and stability established is greatest when it comes from security wrapped in love. With this they are now supported. Tributaries of other streams of culture are flowing in and joining them but they still remain the same stream. Two sets of values now as one lead them to wider, richer and more productive lives. There is hope for the future.

As in all history, everyone does not strive for the top rung of the ladder. Some continue to allow the ridicule of peers to squelch any hope of becoming a would-be leader. Some become despondent when the daily grind of preparation and competition calls for the Indian courage he has lost. Behind the skirt of failure these hide to say, "We'll never make it. They just hire the high-ups." Thus, incentive and contentment went with the old life way, but opportunities are open, where much is being done to redeem mistakes of the past. The feeling of brotherhood goes a long way to repairing the holes in the wall of time. Trust is one of the qualities that will minimize vacillating plans. His history is built on broken promises, causing trust to crumble. In his Indian trust a man was as good as his word. Perfect trust. Why write it down on paper? Many a paper was torn to shreds by broken treaties. Today one of the highest honors is to say "he is a man who keeps his word." Do not ever shatter trust by betraying confidence. When he pours his heart out he does not mean for it to be scattered like feathers in the wind, but for it to be forever sealed by trust. Even a time schedule cut off for apparently more pressing duties or for more important people is taken as a personal offense. Strengthen the Indian through your implicit trust. Even making a possible promise of "maybe I will be able to meet you at seven" means trust to the Apache. It may have not been a definite promise, but to the Indian "maybe" means "for real." If you failed to see this promise completed you betrayed him, and good ground gained is lost, for, "He lied to me. I can't trust him any more."

Mysterious moves of failure of a number of promising leaders may be due to poor communication. Cross-cultural contacts are made daily. This is not a one-way process. In order to understand both parties one must talk and listen. A child may seek comfort from a teacher, . . . "She said my mother has a long nose." The teacher, unaware of the cause for this sobbing, broken heart, may think, "Well, maybe she does." She does not know that is the "bad word," or the worst degradation the child could experience. The underlying element is that there are no vulgar terms in the Apache language, but to make a remark insults the child and lowers his self-image beyond repair. Such similar contacts are made daily by one culture interchanging with another. Thus problems arise and resultant disturbances cause the minority culture to withdraw as within a cocoon, never planning to step out again. This is why the "melting pot" process has failed. Later in life it intensifies a tribal feeling to keep "you" (non-Indian) and "us" (Indian) apart. As he is supported by this cohesive tribalism, the Indian youth ventures into public discourses in defense of his people. Aside from a backbone of tribalism he has the Civil Rights Act of 1968 to strengthen his position. The result is a problem, a so-called Indian problem, but more correctly labeled as a community problem. This needs the understanding and cooperation of the entire community for fair solutions.

This brotherhood policy needs to be communicated to the whole nation. When school children from the East write, "Can you tell me all about all the Indians?" they are lumping them into one pot. "Will you send me a tomahawk, a war club, and a picture of Geronimo?"[d] This child is equipped with only the T.V. symbol of today's American Indian. These questions, multiplied by hundreds, reveal that the larger public is not exposed to reliable information about the oldest minority group.[3] Disappointment waves over the young visitor when he sees only people! While riding on the reservtion I pointed out two riders on fine, roping quarter horses, "There are a couple of Indian cowboys." What a disillusionment for these downcast visitors when these cowboys did not measure up to the "wild west movie" stereotype cowboy. "But where are the cowboys, and where is 'Old Paint'?" one ventured to ask, still not ready to relegate his image to the movies or to a museum piece, and accept the Indian boy as his equal. The Indians only want and need what others have. They want to be equal.

Again different philosophies of culture create variances. Why should a one-room, unpainted cabin be anchored by a triple-duty T.V. antenna, and flanked by a late-model, sporty Mustang? Because that is where the sense of values lies. These new additions create status. With them he feels equal to his Anglo friends. The meager comforts of the humble abode are sufficient, and his community status is not measured by them. It must be understood that these crowded quarters give security, since there is room for each family member. This deep value must not be overlooked. The Indian values will change when they see the worth of change.[4] This clues a non-Indian into better understanding. Visitors refer to the Apache by pointing to his feather. Take the Apache where he is!

Whether the home is this one-room cabin or a modern, seven-room home with a double garage, there are philosophies that remain constant. Upon approaching the Indian he may appear stoical and unmoved. He will not bow before you, because bowing was an act of reverence paid only to the divinity.

Skip introductions; the name isn't important anyway. You will be given a characteristic name such as mine: *Beditcheeglechee'* ("redhead"). Be seated. It is important to accept the place of honor offered you, whether it be the newly upholstered lounger or the choice Pendleton blanket folded over a homemade stool. A visitor implies his superiority in this breach of etiquette. Learn to use even a few words of the Apache language for a speedy rapport. One is really accepted into the family circle when asked to break bread with them. To bind friendship it takes only a cup of coffee or a family feast. Be gracious in accepting their generosity. This the Indians did from the beginning of time.

To refuse this offer places one outside the family. Accept the food without questioning. The meat might be a gift of venison. It might be a gift submitted to the family by a new groom, given as evidence of his determination to display his prowess and become a good provider.

An additional, helpful quality is to be cheerful, to be jovial, and to create a happy atmosphere. Don't enter the home in downcast spirits, as the feeling will bring tears to the family. Likewise, a loud, penetrating voice shows poor training. It will win neither attention nor favor.

Above all, don't be inquisitive. When queried too much the Apache will give you the answer you want, regardless of its validity; anything to get such a rude person off his back. Too many pertinent questions will change a cordial host into the wooden Indian that meets the world outside the doorways of the western novelty shops.

Another way to be accepted is to dress neatly, in the standard style, and thus command a respectful example. To wear jewelry of their handiwork draws the closely knit comment, "Now, you are an Indian."

One treads a dangerous path who pries into family relationships. An illegitimate child may be the subject of discussion. It is not so branded. It belongs to the mother, and holds security in belonging to an acceptable extended family. Devotion to the child never exposes it to scorn or mistreatment. The birth of this child carries no stigma; disapproval is exercised by the abandonment of the child and leaving it to strangers for adoption.

Respect the aged in the home, for they are respected. These four and five generations, united by family ties, constitute the strength of the Indian family. This actuates the Indian culture, or in reality the Indian community.

The steady move to the urban area broke the extended family encampment. Along with it attitudes changed. The houses are arranged in an area where zoning determines the position of the home. No regard is given to the doors, which always opened to the east. Religious ceremonies bow to the east, but in these homes the significance of the east and the new days are crowded out of the lives of the Apaches. Also, with the neighbors all around, who feels like running to the top of the mountain to face the new day in prayer? A large portion of parental control is lost in the split schedules of the working members, and the school or recreational pressures. There is now little place for *it so ye'*, ("grandfather's") tales, or grandmother's opportunity to fulfill her role of directing the lives of the granddaughters.

In despair *itso-ye* shook his head. "It isn't like it used to be. The young people don't listen. They used to obey because they were afraid of the spirits who would witch them if they disobeyed. Now they don't believe in witches and the cheetin's power; so act like wild coyotes."

A radiant glow from past memories goaded him on as he saw the feast grounds of yesterday. "Like the feast, everybody went, they put up their tents and stayed a long time. The young runners did what the two leaders of the relay race asked them to. You know the feast is on the fifteenth.[e] On the night of the fourteenth the boys danced just a little while, then they went to their tent, like the old man said, so they could run good tomorrow." The picture of today's race clouded his countenance. "They just dance all night on the fourteenth. On the fifteenth they are not ready to take their places. They just try to run in their clothes, without dressing in shorts, feathers and paint applied by the medicine man; some, I guess, just run and have 'the bottle' in their pockets while running." The modern rodeo is uppermost in the minds of these young men, who fail to hold the religious significance of the race in their minds or lives.

"The boys don't stay home very much. After they work, they eat in that cafe, and then go rope horses, and then start drinking." Family ties are no longer closely knit where alcoholism intervenes. Thus the family spirit gives way.[6]

While this revolving culture demarcated the attitudes, school, religion and home, the village of Dulce

71

was becoming a community. To approach it at night one could call it a city. The neon, flashing lights attracted attention, the streetlights ran up the side of the mountain, and family lights dotted the valley; it seemed to push the Dulce ridge back to make more room for its ever-expanding borders.

The former sagebrush flats running down to the arroyo were converted into a housing area. By the beginning of this period a Jicarilla Apache housing authority was organized. Individual homes popped up as two- and three-bedroom homes. A twenty-five unit, low-rent housing establishment provided comfortable, respectable, and sanitary homes for the low-income Apaches. The crystal ball has forty more such homes in the planning stage. The community was zoned, streets laid and hard-surfaced. Little Paula's face teemed with pride that broke through the scrubbed-clean look, "Now I can bathe, have clean clothes and be like those other kids because we have water," as she demonstrated the complete water system.

Nineteen sixty-four marked these growths, along with the development of the tribal store into a supermarket. After sixty years the trading post was razed, with many past memories and tall tales buried with it.

Also opportunities were creeping along the horizons and opening into new channels of growth when the Economic Opportunity Act was enacted. Various projects such as education in and prevention of alcoholism, a day care center, and Project Headstart for the oncoming generation, and educational and training opportunities for undereducated adults were instituted. While the nation provided these projects, the Apaches were able to share fully in the benefits of a progressive nation and, like other citizens, were given choices concerning the kind of life they wished for themselves. It broadened their vision, in which incentive had dwindled to the level of the tasks of a day laborer. No longer are they branded "just a herder." Their self-esteem has risen above accepting white man's charity or relief. This prevents America from looking upon them as "wild pets."[7]

They had the security of land; democratic form of government; and now, status. Next came the repeal of sundry statutes, which guaranteed them a right to organize, with the enforcement of cultural and religious liberty. They were again sought out to share their braves in battle. When they returned they needed a "place in the sun." They met challenge in change. A long-range tribal plan organized and united efforts to improve their land. Again the returnee saw his people learning to help themselves, save their land from erosion, and be proud of the land that is theirs. An aerial survey showed his land ribboned with highways, dotted with pumping iron horses and lakes, plus thirteen miles of riverfront for fishing and recreation. His allotment had become a scouting area when his family's sheep dwindled to a handful. Where was he going to place himself in this new world? The Apache had always lived for the day and the pleasures with it. His shifting attitude caused him to look into the future. The future would soon mark a hundred-year life at Dulce. Oh, and the tribe had set up a scholarship fund for furthering education or training for him and others. He was asked to work with recreation and tourism. That must be another new program. He became so overwhelmed with programs, that he wished for many broad brooms to sweep back the surging tide of change. His older sister, a dropout, was attending adult education courses to fulfill her hopes of advanced training. His buddy was off taking vocational training. There were now training centers for Indians. The future held a technical vocational school in Albuquerque. What a maze of changes horded his restless mind. He shouldered his gun, whistled for Old Shep, who followed him to heel along the trail which they both knew. This offered solace and close communion with the spirit, his only comfort.

The voice of the Indian was being heard. It spoke out firmly and quietly. They had organized into a National Council of American Indians. Here the problems, programs and steps of progress are heard annually. This pressure group bids fair to bring results. Birth pains were experienced while the old life-style had to give way, hoping the cooperative aspect of Indian life was being maintained. Reparations for past ills was a cry that was recognized by the Land Claims Act.

With 1970 looming into action the Apache land claims were processed, and industry became a part of Dulce's economic world. An industry at home rather than off in the city will mean more people, healthy economic conditions. The "forward look" is not done hiding with one behind a bush, or freezing dead in his tracks to avoid identity. Each stands up to be counted. On the production line may be one who "harmed my brother," but any foe is forgotten when together individuals work for an honorable wage. The sheep business is one-third of what it was twenty-five years ago, and the cattle business down to one-half as much. The labor force grew in this now-eighteen-hundred-member tribe. It continued to grow steadily, with increased health measures and preventatives.

The year that man stepped on the moon the Apache stepped into technology. Likewise, the horse age gave way to the atomic age, but the Apache has again trotted into the limelight with the ascent of the rodeo for recreation.[8] Also, "Old Paint" has a hard time trying to compete with the Ford Mustang. The move into town is not the government's responsibility nor education. It is the uncontrollable flow of economic life which causes the Apaches to be aware of the color T.V., modern clothing and automobiles. For the Apache, to see is to want. To want means necessity for money. Could he go back to the plow? History may hold memory dear, but can never be repeated. The forward look, the future, is where their sights are set. To be prepared for the future is the cry. The Jicarillas are managing, with relatively slight traumatic consequences, to adapt to the needs of the present commercial system.[9] The dynamic advances from without have combined with the restless energy and boundless resources from within to build a modern reservation — a revitalized reservation.

While the people are on the move to a revitalized life, they are developing to participate wholly in the full American life.[10] This is one of the ten-year tribal goals established. Now there is a sharing of cultural and natural resource wealth with all men for the Apache betterment. Thus may the future see them rich in their ability to share in the enjoyment of life with other human beings.

To some this rapid social change has resulted in social disorganization. The Apache is grappling with this rapid social change, which seems inevitable once the economic base for his former life-style is broken down. So every step taken in the battle against unemployment will be costly in terms of native color and drama. They cannot be taught to make delicate electronic instruments for the space age and simultaneously prevent the sprouting of T.V. antennas from the rooftops.[11]

One industry in which they identify themselves is in the Jicarilla arts and crafts shop, where beadwork, leatherwork and basketwork are their specialties. This has taken them to art displays in Arizona, to the National Indian Art Show in Washington, D.C., as well as points of New Mexico.

The tribal programs and committees are supported by their counterpart, in the Bureau of Indian Affairs. Here the human potential is stressed. Leadership and resource development for the tribe is the agency's trust responsibility. The Apache formerly sat back, saying, "Let the government people do it for me." Now, with this interaction of "outsiders" (meaning state, county and businessmen), they are ready to "get into the saddle" themselves. The greatest hope for Indian progress lies in the emergence of leadership. Into the past goes the leader chained by tribal derision. As the newly appointed personnel director of the JAT Industry said, "Let the people talk. We need tribal leaders. I don't care what they say; I have two ears, so what they say goes in one side and out the other. We need leaders." What's happening to the group-supported leaders? Individuals are stepping out.

This indicator swings around the clock and points to all phases of the culture. Changes are made into consistent, practical patterns for today and tomorrow's life-style. Thus, the culture is an attainment of integrated behavior.

This period of transition is the one of "stepping out." By the close of the century of Jicarilla reservation living the new trails of emergence will be blazed, and that generation will be secure in tribal-paternal support. In this period there are intelligent Indians who drop out of college for emotional reasons. The anxieties are not due to the tribal past, or university present, so much as it is to their fear of the no-man's-land between the two cultures.[12]

Culture change is not only this educational conflict, but the sum of their traits. Culture is the way they live today with yesterday woven into the fiber of life thoughts and actions. We, outside the tribe, may know all about the distribution of the tribes' forms of marriage, mating and rituals, and yet not understand the culture as a whole. Today elements of this culture are used to its own purpose. This purpose he selects from the possible traits, those he can use, and discards those that do not fit into the puzzle of his new world.[13] Other traits today's Apache recasts into conformity with its demands.

This behavior cannot be ignored in the Apache society, nor does it presently monopolize the determined youth. A young Christian leader with broad understanding and interpretation of God's love trembles under a bolt of lightning striking too close for comfort. He seeks the medicine man's services and beseeches his wiles with pollen and prayer to prevent any spell nature might have sent. He can say with the chief of the "Digger"[f] Indians, "In the beginning God gave every people a cup, a cup of clay, and from this cup they drank their life." The figure of speech is full of meaning. Largely, the Apache cup is broken; as Grandpa said, "They don't pay attention to our teachings." With this the shape of meaning of his life is altered. The New Indian is plagued by many problems that beset his ancestors. His life is equipped with sharpened tools of adjustment, so that he can live in today's world and preserve the ethos of his Indian heritage. It is through such cultural autonomy that Apaches can make their richest contribution to American life.[14]

An Apache who wishes to do so may lead a useful and prosperous life in his own Indian environment. He is speaking for himself. The new Indian speaks clearly as his voice rings out his hopes. The hope for his children. He demands a word in his own destiny and is unwilling to settle for less. May the first hundred years of reservation living bring forth Jicarillas who are the new Americans. Their blending of cultures will be woven into an American in America — a greater Indian America. The Apache stock will undergird him. Remember the Apache, a strong people, quick to select and use what suits them from the white man's storehouse, but keeping the essential pattern, society, language, way of life which makes him an Apache. There is no stronger impulse in the Indian than the deep, abiding love for his country.[15] He stood for his nation in time of war. So he stands for his reservation, and the future in plans ahead.

Is this fast-moving stream taking them in the right direction? The older people found it hard to take a quick turn from the former culture. Truly, they have come out of great tribulations, and they wanted to protect their children from similar suffering. That time is past but "Time" continues to keep our memories alive. Doubt clouds their vision as they fail to see there is no need for total assimilation in this turning tide. The remnants of the Apache society are not lost.

At the Indian Youth Council the adventuresome youth were told that people all over the world respected Indians because of what they stood for and the pride they showed, as well as for their integrity, their strength and their great hearts. They are looking to the future leaders as present ones "go down into the West." They want to think of the world as a better place because of its Indians — its Apaches. The world is rocked by insecurity, passion for power and personal advantages. The Indian, the Apache, can slow down the feverish pace of the twentieth-century America. Your wealth lies not in amassed materials but by how much you can share. Apaches have the power to slow down and live as their ancestors.

---

[a] An expression of death. The Apache returns to the Creation by going down into the West.

[b] "Farmer" was the one who maintained this government farm at La Jara district.

[c] 1987 marks the end of the first century of the Jicarilla Reservation.

[d] Geronimo was a chief of the Mescalero Indian tribe.

[e] September 15 is the established date for the Harvest Feast or San Antonio Fiesta.

[f] Digger is a name given by Californians.

Footnotes

CHAPTER 1

1 Phrase from the "Cherokee Memorial to the United States Congress," 29 Dec. 1935.

2 A. B. Thomas, "Jicarilla Apaches," Page 1.

3 Frank C. Lockwood, *The Apache Indians* (New York: Macmillan Co., 1938), page 8.

4 Edward A. Marinsek, "The Effect of Cultural Difference in the Education of Apache Indians" (Ph.D. dissertation, Albuquerque: University of New Mexico), page 4.

5 Ibid., page 4.

6 Ibid., page 5.

7 Ruth Underhill, *Red Man's America* (Chicago: University of Chicago Press, 1953), page 225.

8 Lynn I. Perrigo, *Our Spanish Southwest* (Dallas: Banks, Upshaw & Co., 1960), page 9.

9 Lynn I. Perrigo, *The Rio Grande Adventure* (Dallas: Lyons & Conaham, 1964), page 30.

10 Gordon C. Baldwin, *The Warrior Apache* (Tucson, Arizona: Dale Stuart King, 1965), page 15.

11 "Jicarilla Land Claims Report," page 61 (Santa Fe, New Mexico: National Park Service, 1969), page 5.

12 A. L. Krober, "Cultural and Natural Areas of Native North America," (Berkeley: University of California Press, 1947), page 1.

13 Ibid., page 2.

14 "Jicarilla Land Claims Report," page 10.

15 Notes from interview with Mrs. Joyce Herald, of the Apache Basketry Research Project, Denver University, Denver, Colorado.

16 "Jicarilla Land Claims Report," page 91.

17 Will Levington Comfort, *Apache* (New York: E. P. Dutton & Co., Inc., 1931), page 10.

18 Marinsek, "Effect of Cultural Difference," page 8.

19 Robert S. Reading, *Indian Civilizations* (San Antonio, Texas: The Naylor Co., 1961), page 59.

20 Perrigo, *Rio Grande Adventure*, page 146.

21 F. Stanley, *The Jicarilla Apaches of New Mexico 1540-1940* (Pampa, Texas: Pampa Print Shop, 1962), page 120.

CHAPTER 2

1 Francis E. Leupp, *In Red Man's Land* (Chicago: Fleming N. Revell Co., 1914), from the Foreword.

2 Harry Hoijer and Morris Opler, "The Raid and Warpath Language of the Apache," *American Anthropologist* 42 (1940), page 621.

3 Lockwood, *Apache Indians*, page 618.

4 Frank D. Reeves, *History of New Mexico* (New York: Lewis Historical Publishing Co., 1961), page 20.

5 Stanford Research Institute (prepared for Jicarilla Apache Tribe of New Mexico), "General Background and Tribal Organization," *Needs and Resources of the Jicarilla Apache Indian Tribe*, vol. 1 (Menlo Park, Calif.: Stanford Research Institute, 1958), page 5.

6 Morris Opler, *Myths and Tales of the Jicarilla Apache Indians* (Publication Fund — The Southwest Museum, Los Angeles, Calif.: The American Folklore Society, vol. 1, 1938), page 1. (Reprinted by Kraus Reprint — New York, 1970.)

7 Harry Hoijer, "The Southern Athabaskan Languages," *American Anthropologist* 40 (1938), pages 75-87.

8 F. Stanley, *The Apaches of New Mexico 1540-1940* (Pampa, Texas: Pampa Print Shop, 1962), page 120.

9 Notes from interview with Mr. Laell Vicenti, Apache stockman. Also, F. Stanley, *The Apaches of New Mexico 1540-1940*, page 245.

10 F. Stanley, *The Jicarilla Apaches of New Mexico 1540-1967* (Pampa, Texas: Pampa Print Shop, 1967), page 179.

CHAPTER 3

1 Leupp, *Red Man's Land*, from the Foreword.

2 Ruth Muskrat Bronson, *Indians Are People Too* (New York: Friendship Press, 1944), page 85.

3 Ibid., page 35.

4 Ernest Seton, *The Gospel of the Red Man* (New York: Doubleday & Co., 1956), page 36.

5 Notes from interview with Rev. J. D. Simms, former Dulce missionary.

6 Ibid.

7 Notes from interview with Miss Hendrina Hospers, former Dulce missionary.

8 Notes from interview with Cevero Caramillo, reservation Apache.

9 Edith L. Watson, "Jicarillas, the Happy People," *New Mexico* magazine, December 1945, page 2.

10 Notes from interview with Mr. Laell Vicenti. Also, F. Stanley, *The Apaches of New Mexico 1540-1940*, page 245.

11 Lois Cornell, "The Jicarilla Apache," page 2. (Derived from information provided by her father, Dr. Cornell, the first resident doctor.) A paper.

12 John Collier, *Indians of the Americas* (New York: The New American Library of World Literature, 1961), pages 154-55.

13 Perrigo, *Rio Grande Adventure*, page 255. Also, "Living on the Jicarilla Apache Reservation," a social studies unit by the boarding school and day school on the reservation.

CHAPTER 4

1 E. Russell Carter, *The Gift Is Rich* (New York: Friendship Press, 1956), page 81.

2 The Indian Reorganization Act.

3 Oliver LaFarge, *As Long As the Grass Shall Grow* (New York: Alliance Book Co., 1940), page 97.

4 Bronson, *Indians Are People Too*, page 107.

5 Stan Steiner, *The New Indian* (New York: Harper and Row, Inc., (1968), page 305.

6 Ibid., page 304.

7 Gertrude M. Golden, *The American Indian Then and Now* (San Antonio, Texas: The Naylor Co., 1957), page 45.

8 Information from Garfield Velarde, reservation Apache.

9 Bronson, *Indians Are People Too*, page 133.

10 Steiner, *The New Indian*, page 44.

11 F. Stanley, *The Jicarilla Apaches of New Mexico 1540-1967*, page 315.

[12] Brophy, Aherle, *The Indian* (Norman, Oklahoma: University of Oklahoma, 1966), page 187.

CHAPTER 5

[1] A quotation from the Omaha Tribe.

[2] Jay Monagham, *The Book of the American West* (New York: Simon & Shuster, 1963), page 206.

[3] National Council of American Indians, editorial, *Indian Reservations* 13, No. 2 (1968), page 2.

[4] Notes from First Indian Women's Seminar, Fort Collins, Colorado, 1970, "Indian Values as Opposed to Non-Indian Values" — a lecture.

[5] Notes from interview with Mr. Victor Vicenti, reservation Apache.

[6] Ibid.

[7] Peter Farb, *Man's Rise to Civilization* (New York: E. P. Dutton Co., 1968), page 266.

[8] M. Jourdan Atkinson, *Indians of the Southwest* (San Antonio, Texas: The Naylor Co., 1963), page 198.

[9] Dulce, New Mexico, (newspaper) *Chieftain*, 3 Jan. 1966, page 3.

[10] Ten-year goals established by the Jicarilla Apache Tribe. Dulce, New Mexico, page 16.

[11] Dulce, New Mexico, (newspaper) *Chieftain*, 3 Jan. 1966, page 3.

[12] Steiner, *New Indian*, page 44.

[13] "*The American Indians*," Bureau of Indian Affairs, 1962, from the foreword.

[14] Ibid., page 1.

[15] Seton, *Gospel*, page 37.

Selected Readings

Walter M. Daniels, *American Indians.* New York: H. W. Wilson and Company, 1957.

Jack Shaefer, *New Mexico.* New York: McCann, Inc., 1967.

Morris Opler, *An Apache Life Way.* Chicago: University of Chicago Press, 1941.

Elizabeth M. Page, *In Camp and Tepee.* New York: Fleming N. Revell Company, 1915.

E. E. Dale, *The Indians of the Southwest.* Norman, Oklahoma: University of Oklahoma Press, 1970.

Walter Daniels, *American Indians,* Reference Shelf, Volume 29, No. 4. H. W. Wilson Company, New York, 1957.

Ruth Benedict, *Patterns of Culture.* New York: The

New American Library, Mentor Books, 1959.
Bertha P. Dulton, *New Mexico Indians*. Santa Fe: New Mexico Association on Indian Affairs, 1955.
Jack D. Forbes, *Apache, Navaho and Spaniard*. Norman, Oklahoma: University of Oklahoma Press, 1960.